Spiritual Existential Counseling

Spiritual Existential Counseling

A Path with Heart and Soul

⁝⁞

Randolph Severson

GOLDENSTONE PRESS | *Benson, North Carolina*

Published by Goldenstone Press
P.O. Box 7
Benson, North Carolina 27504
www.goldenstonepress.com

ISBN: 978-0-9907350-0-7

Cover and book design: Eva Leong Casey / Lee Nichol

Cover image, unknown provenance. Due diligence was exercised
in attempting to determine the owner/copyright holder of this image.
Information regarding the image can be sent to the publisher at the address
above; if confirmed, subsequent printings will include attribution.

Printed in USA

GOLDENSTONE PRESS

GOLDENSTONE PRESS seeks to make original spiritual thought available as a
force of individual, cultural, and world revitalization. The press is an integral
dimension of the work of the School of Spiritual Psychology. The mission of
the School includes restoring the book as a way of inner transformation and
awakening to spirit. We recognize that secondary thought and the reduction
of books to sources of information and entertainment as the dominant meaning of reading places in jeopardy the unique character of writing as a vessel
of the human spirit. We feel that the continuing emphasis of such a narrowing
of what books are intended to be needs to be balanced by writing, editing,
and publishing that emphasizes the act of reading as entering into a magical,
even miraculous spiritual realm that stimulates the imagination and makes
possible discerning reality from illusion in the world. The editorial board
of Goldenstone Press is committed to fostering authors with the capacity of
creative spiritual imagination who write in forms that bring readers into deep
engagement with an inner transformative process rather than being specta-
tors to someone's speculations. A complete catalogue of all our books may be
found at *www.goldenstonepress.com*. The web page for the School of Spiritual
Psychology is *www.spiritualschool.org*.

10 9 8 7 6 5 4 3 2 1

For Jacques

"Why does God give us scary thoughts?"

To teach us courage . . .

Contents

᭸

Acknowledgements

To my wife, Sally, my family, and to the many colleagues
and friends whose encouragement has helped bring
these words to fruition, I extend my deepest appreciation.
Special thanks to Goldenstone Press, to the Editor and
Director, Robert Sardello, and to Mr. Lee Nichol for their
understanding and artistry, and for allowing me to retain
on the page the "bardic" and sermonic form in which
these words first took shape in the "craic" of the talking
cure. I am entirely responsible for the departures from
conventional form. With her eye and skills Jocelyn Cha-
fouleas has, once again, given me irreplaceable help. For
a splendid cover, I am indebted to Eva Casey, Lee Nichol,
and Robert Sardello.

Foreword

Here's a concept: the detached analyst, with fashionable beard, rises from behind the couch to enter into dialogue with—whom: the patient? The client? The character disordered? The emotional cripple? The detached analyst, symbol of twentieth-century psychology, finally sees the distressed, the vulnerable, the wounded—not as a case study, but as a fellow pilgrim. Counseled and counselor are both seekers of beauty, truth and goodness in the paradigm of therapy that Dr. Randolph Severson offers in *Spiritual Existential Counseling.*

I first heard Dr. Severson speak years ago at a conference concerning adoption-related issues. As an adopted person struggling with issues of identity and belonging, I heard in the words the ring of truth, accented warmly in a down-home drawl, filtered through ancient Celtic images, and enhanced with powerful literary allusions that have become emblematic of his thought and expression.

What Dr. Severson has done in this concise pioneering work, is to take psychotherapy—what he calls the talking cure—into the new millennium, into the century that Malraux had said would be spiritual, or it would not be. Severson challenges entrenched psychotherapeutic practice and philosophy with the charm and brilliance of a contemporary memoirist. Severson's approach begins with self-identification, a personal revelation that presents his inheritance, his culture, his family, his education, his struggles and sufferings, as the currents which have shaped his identity, as well as his practice of the talking cure. His memoir is daring and endearing, and the reader immediately intuits this is someone to be trusted. Here we have a professed Romantic, a southerner whose words charm as sacraments of hospitality, a dreamer who understands the tasks of listening to other's struggles as a holy privilege, a believer with confident assurance in things he cannot see. Within the framework, Severson evaluates psychotherapeutic philosophy and practice, and introduces what has long been missing—that dimension of the spirit.

As a convert to Catholicism from evangelical religion, Severson also has something to say to Catholicism, which, like psychology, has the potential to become a religion without spirit. Severson offers the priest-theologian von Balthasar as a hinge upon which to turn the door into a new millennium. Beauty, von Balthasar maintained, is the prism through which the other transcendentals of truth and goodness are seen rightly.

As a Catholic priest I am engaged by Severson's take on Catholicism and his appreciation of the richness of the tradition, and am reminded of a criticism of Catholic theology, from none other than Cardinal Schönborn, editor of the *Catechism of the Catholic Church*, when he said that the real situation of theology today is "that of poverty, a lack of greatness, a lack of great inspiration . . . we are in a time of desert." Dr. Severson, for both psychology and theology, is an oasis in that desert. His notion that self-identification is the beginning of effective therapy is also the basis of doing theology—both psychology and theology need to be practiced. Salvation, it is good to remember, comes from the Latin for health.

Severson works toward a reconciliation of religion and science, seeking to overcome the poison of dualist thought (brought into modernity through Calvinist religion) that is largely responsible for the chasm between religion and science, thought and emotion, body and soul. What psychology and religion ought to be about, as von Balthasar would say, is the reconciliation of previously separated parts.

In his introduction to this quite readable work, Dr. Severson sets out, he says, to ravish the reader. He recalls the image of the Annunciation, the dialogue between Gabriel and Mary, and offers it as the great metaphor for the practice of psychotherapy. But, of course, that is as it should be: for what is the Annunciation but conception through intercourse—an intercourse of sound and syllable generated through the mediation of an angel: impregnation through the power of the word as it ravishes the ear and fills the womb with grace. Spiritual Existential Counseling—psychotherapy—the talking cure: the humble appreciation of the power of words to stir, cure, to penetrate our frigidity, empowering us as co-creators of a redeemed but unfinished world.

Permit me, finally, to enter into the hyperbole which Romanticism affords, and paint Randolph Severson as a Gabriel of sorts, an oasis in that desert in which psychology and theology still languish, as one who trumpets the inestimable value of a therapy imbued with spirit, and of a religion re-inspired by beauty.

—Father Thomas F. Brosnan
Blessed Sacrament Catholic Church, Cypress Hills, NY

Spiritual Existential Counseling: an integrative, synthetic approach to counseling based on a phenomenological method and emerging from the phenomenological existential tradition, specifically Catholic Existentialism, though heavily influenced in style and themes by the soul psychology of James Hillman. Critical realist in epistemology, this model is based on a view of human existence as fundamentally "spiritual," that is, primordially oriented to the transcendentals: Truth, Goodness, and Beauty. Similar to narrative therapy in its focus on therapy as conversation and the therapist as expert conversationalist. Distinct, however, in its persuasive (Ciceronian-Christian Humanist) rather than interrogative (Sophistic-Socratic) stance. An activist therapy of statement achieving maximum effects through value and truth memorably and beautifully expressed (eloquence).

Introduction

The style of Berdyaev is definitely different from the style of other Russian writers . . . It is closer to the style of Nietzsche . . . Berdyaev's style produces the impression of energetic vers libre *. . . his prose reminds of jazz.*

—Yakov Krotov

The soul is the task of man.

—Nicholas Gomez-Davila

This book is an exposition of spiritual existential counseling.

Spiritual Existentialism. By spirit I mean "the spirit," the ecstatic dimension of human existence—an upward draft of felt and experienced meaning with a claim upon the human soul. A fire in the belly and the soul. I associate with "spiritual," and, according to the inspiration of the moment, use interchangeably with it, a host of other terms: romantic, passionate, lyrical, heartfelt, prophetic, visionary, inspirational, with heart and soul. By spiritual I mean an orientation that strains to hear what Yeats called "the King's great horn," or Keats a "spiritual ditty of no tone" that believes, again Yeats, in "the Presences that passion, piety, or affection know," in what Faulkner called "the eternal verities," the supernatural virtues of beauty, goodness, unity, and truth that finds, or "spies"—"Look there. Look there," as Lear says, "let us take upon ourselves the mystery of things, as though we were God's spies," that spies in every human life the passionate ingredients for a powerful romance with an eternally happy ending.

By "existentialism" I pay homage to a tradition that affirms the aspirations and drama of the spirit, and often speaks a spiritual language, while simultaneously insisting on the human spirit's anchorage in flesh, history, emotion, culture, and language, in what the existentialist philosopher William Barrett calls "Irrational Man":

> Existentialism seeks to bring (into philosophy) the whole man, the concrete individual in the whole context of his everyday life and in his total mystery and questionableness . . . the man underneath . . . who is born, suffers, and dies . . . the whole or integral man. But the whole man is not without unpleasant things, as death, anxiety, guilt, fear, trembling, and despair . . .

Faulkner and Bernanos are the spirits who hover here: the Bernanos who writes:

> We are created in the image and after the likeness of God because we are capable of loving. Saints have a genius for love . . . the saint is the person who knows how to find in himself, and to make gush forth from the depths of his being, the water of which Christ spoke to the Samaritan woman: "Those who drink of it will never thirst." The water is there in each of us, the deep cistern open under the sky.

And the Faulkner who says:

> I believe that man will not merely endure: he will
> prevail. He is immortal, not because he alone
> among creatures has an inexhaustible voice, but
> because he has a soul, a spirit capable of compas-
> sion and sacrifice and endurance. The poet's, the
> writer's, duty is to write about these things. It
> is his privilege to help man endure by lifting his
> heart, by reminding him of the courage and honor
> and hope and pride and compassion and pity and
> sacrifice which have been the glory of his past.

I call my approach Spiritual Existentialism. I might equally well call it "Hillmanian," so indebted is it, so apprecia-
tive of, so obviously sustained by, the archetypal psychology of James Hillman. Hillman certainly championed
the poetry in man, the afflatus, the inspired imagination,
that I am calling spirit. And Hillman's work was existential in its recognition of what he would call *Ananke*, the
Underworld, the Brood of Night, that is to say, human
finitude. As a "physician of culture" and "psychologist of
ideas," in his exultant lyricism, and in the dazzle of his
wordplay Hillman often seems more akin to Kierkegaard
and Nietzsche than Jung; to Berdyaev and Unamuno
more than Neumann or von Franz, Edinger, or Giegerich;
and he wasn't just akin, but kin to Binswanger. Yet in
biography and affiliation, Hillman was a "Jungian." This
work, however, aligns itself not with Hillman the "Jungian Analyst" but with Hillman the "Therapist to the
Men's Movement," as the *New York Times* eulogized him,
that is, with an activist, interventionist, skaldic, bardic—
dare I say it?—*shamanistic* form of therapy as in "The

analyst listens. The Shaman *speaks.*" So, too, does the orator, the Humanist. So, too, does the spiritual existential counselor. In this sense, this book could be said to develop an as-yet-undeveloped aspect of archetypal psychology, an aspect, I would argue (see appendices) more in keeping with its animating provenance and truth.

The method of existential phenomenology, a style of descriptive amplification, a going over and over, "playing it again, Sam" style that pursues truth through a "critical naiveté" that tries to "know" any phenomena by attending to it as it is given, in the way that it is given, prior to any assignment of meaning or imposition of explanation or interpretative scheme. Phenomenology arrives at truth not through a violence of abstraction that produces mental pictures or abstract concepts of formulations in the mind that "correspond" to reality, but through an ongoing engagement with reality out of whose interplay and dialogue truth emerges as a diaphanous blast, or gradual, progressive, almost seductive illumination.

To present spiritual existentialism as a path for counseling is the goal here. The journey divides into three stages. First, we address the counselor's identity.

The first chapter describes my identity as a counselor, or what Jung calls "my personal equation."

By subtitling this book "A Path with Heart and Soul," I mean to take sharp issue with the mistaken notion that a counselor's model or skills are more important than his humanity, and to suggest that counseling is less a short-term problem-solving meeting between a service provider and a consumer, or doctor and patient, or an expert and a client, or a professional with a lay person, than it is what existentialism would call an "I-Thou" encounter, a long-term encounter between human beings, individual people, with their own foibles, stupidities, flaws, dreams, agonies, desires, and aspirations.

Being the kind of counselor I am makes me loathe to present any definition of what the personal or professional identity of any counselor "should" be, and I would much rather simply tell you who I am, and how things appear to me, while hoping that you will hear me out, and perhaps, as you read, you will think on these things with me, then, afterwards, on your own.

To do so, of course, I have to overcome my hesitation and trepidation about telling you who I am, about wondering what you'll think, or even if you'll be very much interested. Won't this bore you? Will you think I'm crazy? Am I really important enough, valuable enough, interesting enough that anyone would be willing to sit for an hour and just listen to "me on me," "me explaining me?" Wouldn't it be better to just keep it to myself? Endure? Suffer through? Protect my privacy? My anonymity? I'm afraid I'd be embarrassed. Dare I risk it?

I dare. But only because hour after hour, day after day, this is exactly what I ask and hope my clients will do, and what I encourage and try to inspire them to do. And what's good enough for the goose . . . as they say. Or better said, I owe them at least once, an example of the courage they routinely show.

In Chapter 2, I try to initiate a phenomenological return to "things themselves" in counseling. I ask for and try to instance an effort to think and talk about counseling in the way that we think and talk in counseling. The current gap in "style in theory" the professional literature (and communication with Managed Care Providers) and "style in practice" is killing counseling, putting too much of a strain on counselors as they try to conceptualize in one way, consistent with abstractions of theory that they have seen diagrammed in books, or the categories and "treatment plans" required by managed care, while responding to clients in a completely different way, one that is vivid and concrete enough to be memorable and promote change. The levels of description and meaning are not identical, but meaning ought to be at the horizon of description, an illumination and emergence from within it, not something imposed from without or made in substitution of the density of the real.

Third, I will try to sustain this effort by locating within the experience of counseling the "horizon" that will allow me to develop theories of change, personality, neurosis, etc. without transcending the phenomenon in a way that would abandon it or make it something other than it is in the terms that it is typically experienced.

A word here, with eyes on the floor, so to speak, about my "style." The first time I was ever invited to speak on a national stage it was on the basis of a recommendation made by a colleague who had been impressed by an audiotape I had done, and described me to the conference organizers as someone who did "a great wizard act." To my enormous chagrin I found myself described as Randolph "The Wizard" Severson in the conference program. I feared that the audience would expect me to juggle and perform a few card tricks and a pull a rabbit out of a hat.

I think that what my colleague was trying to express, was the fact that the way I present, indeed the way I think and talk, diverges from what is considered "proper," as my grandmother would say, or "appropriate" as we counselors would say, among professionals. Unlike most of my colleagues, I'm an intuitive, not a systematic thinker. In terms of logical consistency and clarity I can't compete with most of my colleagues. I'm too flowery and fantastic, and too undisciplined to ever write a textbook, and too idiosyncratic, too much the romantic self-indulgent dinosaur to ever chance into best-sellerdom.

As one of my mentors once put it, "When I read you I get very impatient for you to get to the point . . . but then I catch your rhythm and your imagery catches me. You write those 'self-consuming artifacts' that Stanley Fish talks about. After I finish reading I can't remember exactly what you said, but I find myself thinking about your topic in slightly different terms."

I do, I think, have a gift of words and a courage and sincerity of emotion and vision whose impact may inspire you. I do sometimes find the right words, and as a counselor, help others find them with me—and when you find them, when the soul shines through even the simplest phrase, or some fleeting expression compresses into it a whole universe of previous felt but inarticulate meaning, it's like church bells ringing in the heart. The world turns, the earth moves, or more usually, something shifts, oh so slightly, inside. You feel better, you grow, you grow closer to your loved ones, to others, maybe to God, you know what to do. Growing in the spirit is what I'd call it. It's not about being a good writer; it's about being a good witness. It's not about communication skills. It's about loving and then trying to count the ways.

To do it though, you've got to throw your heart out in front of you, wear your heart on your sleeve, be willing to be the fool, like Parsifal, the knight whose name means "pierced to the heart."

I've been pierced to the heart a time or two. How about you?

An additional word about the sporadically odd layout. It's not just affectation. For reasons that will become clear, I think it is incumbent upon anyone who "writes" about counseling to at least make some effort to communicate the modulations of the voice. To refuse to do it betrays— or so I would argue—the nature of our work, which is, after all, a "talking cure." Hence I have tried as best I can to match the impression that these words will make upon your eye, to the impression that they might make upon your ear were I talking to you. My further authority for this is the things that I have actually known and loved— known and loved most when it comes to "writing." And that would be, first *The King James Bible*, Red Letter Edition, whose typographical improvisation reduces even the boldest de-constructivist or post-modernist to the status of a schoolboy trying hard to stay within the lines. Second, it's in payment of a debt to the lyrics printed on old blues, and rock and roll album covers, over which

I pored as a boy and continue to pore now that I am a man. Their ragged, casual lyrics and eccentric punctuation have taken me even deeper into a spiritual identification with the soul of the music.

I once attended an Ericksonian workshop where the trainer began by asking the audience if they were willing to be enchanted. I plan to enchant you, dear reader.

I want to ask for what Coleridge, like any good hypnotist prepared to cast a spell, called your "willing suspension of disbelief," but my ambitious heart vaults over that—

I want to ravish you—

like Dürer's painting of the Blessed Virgin being impregnated by the Holy Spirit through the ear, 'a sacred image of words'—a sacred image of words—potential, creative, redemptive impact on the spirit.

So now, let me ravish you, if I can, so that, as Yeats said, in association with an image of another "annunciation": "we can put that knowledge on."

CHAPTER ONE

IDENTITY

. . . I do dislike contributing more such egocentric tales; but I shall try to do it in a classical style, by making some point out of the stories, using them as the rabbis did and the Catholic fathers and the Eastern sages and monks.

—James Hillman

How we hear patients depends very much on how we have formed our own biography. Therefore, I think it very important, if we want to listen consciously, to be conscious about the narrative, the kind of story we put ourselves in.

The most critical factor in counseling from my point of view is the counselor's identity. Maslow recognized that the concept of identity comprised existential psychology's most meaningful contribution. He writes:

> First of all, permit me to define existentialism in a personal way, in terms of "what's in it for me." To me it means essentially a radical stress on the concept of identity and the experience of identity as a *sine qua non* of human nature and of any philosophy or science of human nature.

In existentialism, identity is determined by our "situatedness," which refers to multiple factors and our response, from the freedom of our personhood, to them. For me, an extremely fruitful means for reflecting on the theme of identity is the literary critic Kenneth Burke's idea that the great literary genres of epic tragedy, comedy, romance, and satire are not only literary categories, but also what he calls "strategies for living," that is, forms of psychological identity, fundamental orientations to reality. This implies that the study of literature is valuable for understanding psychology and counseling, and, reflexively, that the insights yielded by psychology might sophisticate appreciation of literary works. In *Healing Fictions* James Hillman arrives at and explicates both notions.

"Situatedness" I assess in terms that I call "the elementals," which I learned not from a book on existential psychology, but through my own history and the affections and admirations of love. When I was a boy I spent a lot of time with my grandfather, who for his time and place was a sizeable landowner for whom, at various times, many folks worked—ranch-hands, hay bailers, loggers, fence builders, tenants, tenant farmers, hunters who wanted access to his land. When my grandfather sized up a fella, what he wanted to know was where you were born? Who were your people? What church did they belong to? What kind of work were you good at, and what you had learned from it? What he mainly wanted to know about your "learning" was whether or not you realized and were prepared to live that way—to live in a way that showed you knew that you had to respect and care for the land if you wanted it to care for you, that you had to give something, as it were, and couldn't just wear it out and move on.

I think this was a pretty good way of "assessing" folks. It told him what he wanted to know without humiliating those over whom he was exercising a great deal of power, and it enabled him to truly get to know and respect those who worked for and depended on him.

My own adaptation of this method is that when I "assess" a client I want to know—What's your history and what meaning does it have to you? And how has that meaning changed? And how does it change, if any, with perhaps new "facts" emerging as we talk? I want to know what someone identifies with. Is it other people—concrete loyalties and affection for them? Is it abstract ideals, images, symbols, or rituals? Or is it concrete judgments gleaned from their own experience? What are their core existential and spiritual beliefs? What kind of work do they do; what do they like and don't like about it? Is it a vocation or a job? And what have they learned from it—learned from their work, since this is how most of us spend the greater part of each day, that is, at work, not at home; and learned from relationships—the intimacies, risks, joys, and disappointments of human love—about the ultimate meaning of life? And what do they think is their responsibility in terms of "giving back?"

This form of "assessment" gives me not only the information that any counselor would want in terms of development, family of origin issues, affect, imagery, cognition, behavior, etc., it also allows me to genuinely get to know this new "colleague" in the counseling experience that I call my "client." It gives me a chance to get to know another human being in a way that most of us don't allow ourselves to be known or to get to know another, in part because we don't know how, while in part because we're afraid to risk it.

Now if a counselor's identity is so critical, even decisive, in effective psychotherapy, I think the best place to begin my description of spiritual existential counseling is with a description, or more descriptively said, evocation of my own identity as a therapist. In other words, I'm going to do an "existential elemental" assessment of myself, a psychosocial assessment if you will, in terms both of literary genre and by asking myself the same questions hazarded by my grandfather—where I was born, who are my people, what church I belong to, what is my work and what have I learned from it?

Burke and my grandfather—

These two men, now both dead and gone, Kenneth Burke, whose wisdom lives on through his books, and my grandfather, whose wisdom lives on now through these words of mine.

So who am I? What is my identity?

I am a romantic. A romantic. This shouldn't surprise you. In outlook, existentialism and romanticism are closely aligned; across a century and a half they echo each other. As Lucia Radl observes:

> Both the Romanticists and Existentialists ac-
> centuate freedom and oppose conventions. Both
> schools oppose the rationalism of preceding
> generations and give free scope to emotions, to
> intuition, to imagination. They find alike affinity
> in mysticism, and both advocate a return to reli-
> gion . . . Both schools stress human individuality,
> and decry technical progress. (Lucia Radl, "Existen-
> tialism and Adlerian Psychology" in *Essays in Individual
> Psychology*, ed. Kurt Adler and Danica Deutsch, New
> York: Grove Press, 1959.)

I've added "spiritual" to existentialism" as fitting for my "model" in order to highlight its romantic aspect and background.

Yes, I'm a romantic. I have to be.

I'm a romantic. Yes, I'm a romantic.

I have to be: I'm a Texan, a son of Texas, of Sam Houston, "the hero of Texas history" who in fact and form and figure bestrides the state as a colossus, and whose Woodlands Home, and the Steamboat House, where he died, I visited many times as a boy, and in whose honor my wife and I named our first born son . . .

Houston, who bore the bloodline of a Norman knight and "whose ancestors were in the company of Scottish archers that led the way for Jeanne d'Arc from Orleans to Reims," admired by the politician Kennedy as a profile in courage, and by William Carlos Williams, poet, as the ideal of rooted and renewed American manhood. "It is imperative that we sink." Houston, the "Big Drunk," whose soul drank at the fountain of the Wilderness, of his years among the Cherokee, the Sam Houston of whose happiest days he wrote: "along the banks of streams, side by side with some Indian maiden, sheltered by the deep woods, making love and reading Homer's *Iliad*," the Houston whose character was formed by a romantic play about the Scottish Highlands: As James A. Michener says in *The Eagle and the Raven,* " . . . the Nashville play that created the deepest impression on Houston, helping form his attitudes toward honor, self-deportment, and public oratory . . . was John Home's

Douglas, a histrionic masterpiece of the Scottish Highlands . . . 'Like Douglas conquer, or like Douglas die!' . . . each night he heard this stirring line, this avowal of honor, and its rhythm became part of his arsenal." The Houston who died: "As the slanting shadows of sunset crept upon Steamboat House, General Houston ceased to breathe. A Life so strange and so lonely, whose fingertips had touched stars and felt them change to dust, had slipped away."

> Margaret asked God to make her children men and women worthy of their father. From her husband's finger she removed the talisman that fifty years before another mother had given a boy soldier to confront the world. Margaret held the ring so that the children might see graven on its inner surface the short creed that Elizabeth Houston said must forever shine in the conduct of her son. It was "Honor." (Marquis James, *The Raven*)

I have to be: I'm a Southerner. It is sometimes said that the Civil War was caused by too many Southern young bloods reading Byron and Scott by candlelight, and dreaming of love and glory.

Whether you talk about the origins of the South in Jamestown and the romance between an English adventurer, John Smith, and the Indian Princess, Pocahontas.

Or in the lost colony at Roanoke, Sir Walter Raleigh's dreams: Raleigh—poet, historian, courtier, financier, mystic, statesman, soldier, lover who lost his head in the tower.

Jamestown and Roanoke, Virginia—Virginia named for
the Virgin Queen, Spenser's fairy queen.

Whether it's gone with the wind, mint juleps, magnolias
and walking through an arbor of trees by moonlight.

Whether it's Rhett Butler and Miss Scarlet, or General
Andrew Jackson and his beloved Rachel.

Whether it's Huck and Jim lazily floating down the Mis-
sissippi listening to bullfrogs and counting the stars.

Whether it's our generals, General Jeb Stewart, as
Faulkner says, "his plumed hat in his hand and his
long tawny locks, tossing to the rhythm of his speech,
appeared as gallant flames smoking with the wild and
self-consuming splendor of his daring" or George Patton,
with his poetry, his profanity, and pearl-handled pistols.

Or our writers, Faulkner, Thomas Wolfe, James Dickey.

Whether it's Harlequin or Hollywood.

Whether it's *Gone with the Wind*, *Band of Angels*, *Raintree
County*, *Breakfast at Tiffany's*, or *Home From the Hills*.

Whether it's lost cause or rebel yell.

Eat a peach, free bird, green river or the King and Graceland.

The soul of the South, rising above even the evil of slavery, lynch mobs, cross burnings, Church bombings or

the infernal cadences of "Segregation now, segregation tomorrow, segregation forever" is, as Harper Lee wrote, and as Gregory Peck, Atticus with that mellifluous deep river resonated voice, says in the movie made from Miss Lee's book—the soul of the South is the mockingbird, and it's a sin to kill a mockingbird.

> That was the only time I ever heard Atticus say it was a sin to do something, and I asked Miss Maudie about it.

> "Your father's right," she said. "Mockingbirds don't do one thing but make music for us to enjoy. They don't eat up people's gardens, don't nest in corncribs, they don't do one thing but sing their hearts out for us. That's why it is a sin to kill a mockingbird."

Hello, Mr. Bluebird. Freebird. The mockingbird, cousin to the English nightingale. "I cannot see what flowers are at my feet," said Keats, but I reckon they be Indian paintbrush or bluebonnets.

As I'm a Southerner by birth, I'm Celtic by cultural heritage. All Southerners are. In fact there has been a wealth of interesting features done about how deeply Celtic Southern culture is. Celtic culture takes many shapes: Anglo-Celt and Afro-Celt, Scots and Irish, Welsh, Cornwall, Brittany in France, Galicia in Spain. But although a Southerner born and bred, I never really felt the Celtic flame so keenly as one late January when I flew in a snowstorm into the Newark airport and then later in the evening slipped and slid my way up a frozen street and stepped into a Morristown, New Jersey, Irish, working-class bar. All the men looked like me, younger or older versions. No one was going to make fun of curls and fair skin in this bar. And the women—the women, eyes the color of the sea, dark hair flecked with gold or red, skin like foxglove blooming in the snow—these were the women who had walked through my poetry and dreams, the dark beer flowing, the meal as heavy on the meat as when the Red Branch ruled, and Fergus got drunk, and Cuchulian killed Ferdia at the cattle ford, the tenor sax, mystic, Celtic blues, love drunk rumble and wail of Van Morrison on the jukebox. It was a homecoming for me. *Tír na Nog*, pure heaven.

Or, to steal a phrase from Van Morrison, "the viaducts of my dream."

Celtic, then, the skirl of the bagpipes, heather and the gloaming, Finn and Cuchulian, the west of Ireland, the Highlands, the Welsh Mountains where Owen Glendower disappeared, his banner of a golden dragon on a white field waiting to be raised again, six nations, one soul, Ireland, Scotland, Cornwall and Wales, Mann and Brittany, the Wales of Dylan Thomas, "Now as I was young and easy under the apple bough," "A Child's Christmas in Wales;" or the great Welsh divines, mounting their *hwyl*. "This word, as used in its preaching connection, cannot be translated. Strictly, *hwyl* is Welsh for a sail of a ship, but in its religious sense the term is used to describe the exaltation that descends on a minister during a sermon or prayer so that he is carried away into flights of singing or chanting oratory. He is lifted on a great wind, as it were, and charges triumphantly about in a stormy ocean of words."

The Scotland of Hugh McDaniel—

> Here is the real Scotland,
> The Scotland of the leaping salmon,
> The soaring eagle, the unstalked stag,
> And the leaping mountain hare . . .

Yeats' Ireland—

> We were the last romantics—chose for theme
> Traditional sanctity and loveliness;
> Whatever's written in what poets name
> The book of the people; whatever most can bless
> The mind of a man or elevate a rhyme;
> But all is changed, that high horse riderless,
> Though mounted in that saddle Homer rode
> Where the swan drifts upon a darkening flood.

A word more about this Celtic attitude since nearly everything I have to say presupposes it.

As I am a romantic because I'm Celt, so perhaps I see "Gaeldom" through rose-colored glasses, a Celtic twilight sensibility. Too much Yeats and A.E. Too much Stevenson and Scott, but that would be the Southern way to do it—wouldn't it? By candlelight. But I have tried to temper that by dropping anchor in the solid, authoritative scholarship of John Prebbles whose objective but vivid account of the golden age of Celtic culture in Glencoe, Scotland is invaluable.

Glencoe! Glencoe! Bring me my bow of burning gold. Come walk with me and talk with me in the early morning when the sun comes shining through—on the Celtic ray, like Van Morrison says. Walk with me, talk with me, beside the glittering streams and through the heather.

At one time I would have felt the need to introduce these lengthy passages with more explanation and context, fearing that presenting them in isolation would be equivalent to presenting them in a vacuum in which they would appear as strange and exotic as a glowing piece of moonstone falling from the sky.

But something changed in the '90s—a Second Celtic Renaissance, whose influence lingers today.

What changed was the explosion of Celtic history, symbols, politics, and dance, into pop and popular culture, and the group mind which is never fully conscious of itself, but plays continually over and into consciousness like muzak at the grocery store. There were the *Highlander* movies and TV show; the movies *Braveheart, Rob Roi, Michael Collins, The Devil's Own*, with Brad Pitt mimicking a Belfast accent; there's the phenomenal popularity of *The Lord of the Dance* appearing just about everywhere; the book *How the Irish Saved Civilization* on the bestseller list week after week; there was a definite increase in the influence of traditional Celtic music on rock and popular music, the Chieftains co-record with as many other artists as John Lee Hooker, etc. The TV shows, the movies, the music, the dance, the sweep of the scenery in the film, the excitements of the drama, the inspiration and emotional identifications of the music and scores, the hypnotic appeal of Celtic dance, built as it is upon the escalating tension of powerful sexual and aggressive energies rigidly constrained—all of these together, whether you're familiar with all of these productions or just a few of them—together create a shared frame of reference upon which I'd like to call as the background against which you might contemplate these descriptions.

The Celtic world rose most recently to magnificence and pinnacle at Glencoe during the seventeenth century. As Prebble writes:

> In the seventeenth century the Highland way of life reached its zenith and began its bright fall to extinction. The people of Glencoe, like most in the mountains, felt no sympathy for the outside world. Though they would range far to steal cattle or sell their own, to fight as mercenaries or join in wars that promised but never brought a return of Clan Donald's power, the Valley of the Dogs was enough for them. It was the country of the Feinn and the home of the Saints. If wild boar and wolf were now gone, it was still the land of marten and wildcat, of fox and badger. Eagle and kite swam in the currents above Aonach Eagach. There were red deer on Rannoch. Linnet and thrush sang with blackbirds in the oaks at Achnacone, and larks climbed above the stillness of Achtriachtan. On the meadows in spring were primroses and hyacinths. By the river grew cherry and willow, elderberry and briar. The west winds brought swans from the Outer Isles to feed on water weeds in the river pools. Herring were silver-bright in Loch Leven, and above them hung the sails of ships from Ireland and France. "Traveler, you are welcome here" was the people's greeting to those who came in friendship.

During the evenings the people danced and sang and told tales. They listened to the pipers and to the many poets of Clan Iain Abrach, enriching their spirits and refreshing their hearts . . .

It was believed in the Highlands, and particularly by the MacDonalds themselves, that all men of Glencoe were poets from birth, and it was said that if one of them could not readily put his tongue to verse when invited then his paternity was open to doubt. In a country without any substantial written culture, where oral tradition jealously preserved was the inspiration of life, this glorious claim probably had some truth in it. The spirit of man is instinctively poetic, seeking expression in imagery, and only an age that has abdicated its emotions to professionals has forgotten this. If Glencoe in the seventeenth century was not a nursery of poets, they were certainly made welcome there, and paid for their board with the rich coin of their verse. Ordinary men touched poetry in the names they gave to the land in which they lived. A rock on the north wall was the Anvil of the Mist, a black tarn where they once fought over the division of cattle was the Little Loch of Blood, and a burn rising musically from the earth was the Water of the Singing Birds. For all things in their way of life, the savagery and the sweetness, they sought an immortality in verse, but most of it died when their voices were stilled . . .

And the people of Glencoe were also Catholics.

This world of dignity and beauty, poetry and swordsmen, this traditional and Catholic world was destroyed by three great hammer blows from its enemies: the massacre at Glencoe of the great Clan Donald, "the brilliant pillars of green Alba," as the poet says, who were the defenders and custodians of the ancient traditions of the Gael, the debacle of Culloden and the defeat of glorious Bonnie Prince Charlie, Charles Stuart, who had the whole world in his hands but then dropped it, and finally the Highland Clearances when the poor were forcibly removed from the land by the lairds, the owners to whom they were immemorially bound by ancient and feudal customs of mutual obligation, so that the available acreage could be more readily and profitably exploited.

With the extirpation of the culture of the Celt, spirits of beauty and meaning perished. The *sidhe*, ghost-dancing spirits. Cuchulian. But only the fool who believes that history advances through the straight, successive point-by-point linear progression of the line rather than the deepening and encompassing reversions of the spiral, the archetypal Celtic motif, would reject the possibility of revival.

Braveheart—do you remember the part at the end about Scotland, the Gael, the Celts, being "a nation of warrior-poets?" It was probably not so far from the truth, but as with the Sioux or Cheyenne, it's probably not so far from the truth about any traditional culture where the drama and energy of passion, the poetry of the heart, the civilities of tribal domesticity, and the pastoral beauty of a life attempted to be lived in communion with the earth, the sky, and the cycle of all the seasons, have not departed.

Like the Celt, the Gael, like the men of Glencoe. I'm also Catholic. I became Catholic so I could remain a romantic, so my romanticism could be fulfilled, so I could, with good reason, right reason, *recta ratio*, reason intact, believe with Blake, "that Israel's tents do shine so bright"; with Shelley that love is the basis of all morals; with Keats that "truth is beauty, and beauty truth"; with Wordsworth, that the divine rolls through even the trivial, the lowly, and the commonplace; with Coleridge that sin, contrition, penance, and forgiveness can bring a healing so immense that all creation from its eyes is beautiful, even the beasts of the deep, whether Leviathan or sea snakes, and that we can bless them unawares; and with Byron, yes, Byron even, for few verses, it seems to me, resonate with a richer, eminently Catholic sensibility than these lines of Byron, where the poet in the guise of his character Don Juan, subordinates the pleasure associated with metaphysics and science in their shared contemplation of the cosmos as a perfectly constructed harmony to the beauty of his lady's eyes.

> He thought about himself, and the whole earth,
> Of man the wonderful, and of the stars,
> And how the deuce they ever could have birth;
> And then he thought of earthquakes, and of wars,
> How many miles the moon might have in girth,
> Of airballoons, and of the many bars
> To perfect knowledge of the boundless skies;
> —And then he thought of Dona Julia's eyes.

I became a Catholic to believe that human passion and romance, with their fever and blues—"you give me fever," says the old rock and roll song—prefigure and analogically reflect a divine passion from whose eternal romance with us the thrill is never gone.

I became a Catholic so I could believe that truth is best expressed, not in the definitions and logical distinctions of prose, nor in the refinements of aesthetically perfect poetry, but in rhapsody that strains to praise.

I became a Catholic to believe that the glory of God is most limpidly glimpsed in the human being who is fully alive.

I call myself a Hans Urs von Balthasar Catholic, of whose work I am a clumsy, but enthusiastic exegete. Cardinal von Balthasar, a Catholic theologian, was a contemporary of Barth and Rahner. A Swiss, an ex-Jesuit, he worked for most of his career in collaboration with Adrian von Speyr, a mystic, to whose own writings von Balthasar felt himself deeply joined and indebted. A German-speaking Swiss, his original field of scholarship was German culture, rather than philosophy or theology, and he associated himself with the poetic, aesthetic tradition of Goethe rather than Hegel or Kant.

Because his major works, most impressively the multi-volume *The Glory of the Lord*, have only been recently translated from the original German, von Balthasar is not widely known outside of professional Catholic theological and philosophical circles, although in addition to his professional theological work, he wrote tons of devotional and pastoral literature. In fact, the man was unbelievably prolific. Take the combined works of Freud, Jung, and Heidegger, stack them up on a table, then next to them stack von Balthasar's output, and the von Balthasar pillar will topple over quickest because the books are piled so much higher. A legitimate criticism of von Balthasar's writing it that it is too verbose, but this verbosity, with its distinctive expressive flourishes, is conscious, an expression of theological convictions, and a sharp rebuke to modern stylistic conventions with their journalistic reduction of standards to voiceless uniformity. Von Balthasar is a romantic and rhapsodist in style, which is one of the reasons I adore him. But questions of style aside, it is the theological brilliance and content of his work that brought him the Cardinal's hat, praise from even Cardinal Ratzinger, as "the most cultured man in Europe," and finally, the stunning epithet, now often applied to his name, "the glorious doctor," as St. Thomas is "the common doctor," of the Catholic Church.

Von Balthasar's central notion is beauty. He grieves its passing from the world: "Beauty is the disinterested one . . . a word which both imperceptibly and yet unmistakably has bid farewell to our new world, a world of interests, leaving it to its own avarice and sadness."

And he yokes his extraordinary effort to the task of re-installing beauty into the heart of the Catholic Faith. For him, beauty is the seal of the other great transcendentals:

> As the last transcendental, the beautiful guards
> the others and sets the seal on them, without the
> light of grace which is freely bestowed. And a
> Christianity which went along with modernity and
> subscribed merely to the true (faith as a system of
> correct propositions) or merely to the good (faith
> as that which is most useful or healthy for the
> subject) would be a Christianity knocked down
> from its own heights.

The entirety of von Balthasar's output coheres in terms of beauty. It is the rock upon which he builds his theology.

I call myself a von Balthasar Catholic because of beauty. I too believe in beauty as a path to God and certainly to healing. But it's not only von Balthasar's philosophy that interests me; it's his anthropology, his psychology as well, as developed in his *Man in History*. As a Christian, von Balthasar believes that God is love, and since the language of love is poetry, then the Christian is called to be a poet. He writes:

> The Christian has the privilege of remaining to the end, and in everything he does, a "poet." In the eyes of the children of this world he is a dreamer, not in the sense that he lacks the discipline of the Church and falls into childishness, but in the sense that he has a youthful enthusiasm for the model which he has discovered and which he makes the idol of his heart.

And not only a poet, but forever "a youth of a thousand summers"—a phrase from Blake, or is it Van Morrison?

> It is just at this point that the Word of God reveals his eternal, youthful power. He is youthful by nature; he does not simply put one into an enthusiastic mood which will pass. He imparts substantially that Spirit that makes all things new. It is, inseparably, also the Spirit of Jesus who was always young . . .

Growing old can be a humanly rich and dignified experience, but it cannot, strictly speaking, be called specifically Christian.

What keeps him (the Christian) young is the youthfulness of the Word of God. That is the flame that blazes in the Gospels and prevents the world of Christ from ever being completely at home in the disenchanted world of grown-ups. Does not the Sermon on the Mount, with its utopian, uncompromising idealism, appear odd among all the other ethical systems of mankind? Do not the moralists have to adapt it a little and interpret it *ad usum delphini* in order to make it acceptable for ordinary people? "This disclosure is to be understood in a spiritual, figurative sense, that is, as oriental hyperbole!"

And finally those flaming speeches of St. Paul:

Christianity established itself in the world at that time, which did not lack maturity, virility, and strength, on the basis of its youth, simply because Christians were in their being always a generation younger than everyone who surrounded them, and persecuted them. Like boys who throw away their lives recklessly and without counting the cost, for the sake of an adventure that is fun, they faced death. Youth is used to conquering.

The specifically Christian virtues, idealism, altruism, romance, eros, joy, and love, are the virtues of summer before the leaves of autumn fall. Von Balthasar legitimizes the outlook of youth as specifically Christian.

A theologian who celebrates beauty as a path, poetry, and the idealism and eros of youth. A Catholic theologian who recognizes phenomenology's significance for our age and insists that Christianity must make Heidegger's project its own, is an authority to whom a spiritual existential counseling can look to for illumination and guidance. That's my kind of theologian.

I'm a Catholic because I believe in the stories . . .

Father Andrew Greeley describes Catholicism as first and foremost "a congeries of stories." And that's what my faith most certainly is to me, a gospel of stories existing pre-consciously, settled in my soul quite comfortably to determine probably nearly everything I think and believe, and probably occasioning my most intimately and deeply felt emotions.

In part these stories are religious, and some are drawn from romance and folk tales, stories of saints and miracles, but at the deepest levels, that is, when the bucket plops down into the deepest wells of my soul, what you find are the stories from the Bible, memorized as a bible-toting boy in a Bible-based Church, long before I converted to Catholicism.

And what these stories tell me, these stories about Samson, King David, and finally Christ and his disciples, whom he made fishers of men, Samson and Delilah and the jawbone of an ass, and the bees that poured from the lion carcass, David, the shepherd boy slaying Goliath, and playing his harp for the King, about the birth of the baby Jesus, the shepherds and the wise men, the baptism by John the Baptist, the temptation in the desert, healing the sick, raising the dead, preaching to the five thousand, the Last Supper, Crucifixion and Resurrection, is that God is like me, and that he cares about me personally, but that he is greater than me, and that I should strive to be like him, and that I do so by increasing in wisdom, but most of all love—faith, hope, and love; faith, hope, and charity, as St. Paul describes the super-natural virtues in those miraculously beautiful verses about how, though I speak with the tongue of angels but have not love, I am nothing.

What I also take from Greeley is the fact that in these just-repeated sentences about God he would change the pronoun from He to She. Greeley insists that it is the really distinctive mark of the Catholic faith that God loves us as a mother loves her child, not in a stern, forbidding, judgmental, punitive way, but with an all-embracing, all-forgiving love. Greeley writes:

> The Catholic imagination sees God and Her grace lurking everywhere and hence enjoys a more gracious and benign repertory of religious symbols than do most other religions . . . Catholics consistently have more "gracious" images of God: they are more likely than others to picture God as a Mother, a Lover, a Spouse, and a Friend (as opposed to a Father, a Judge, a Master, and a King).

How this emphasis on the feminine nature of the divine and divine love translates psychologically for me is in a renewed appreciation of the place of women in the Gospels, and the place of those faculties and functions of the mind and human nature that we customarily either

imagine as feminine or associate with living women.
I mean most fundamentally feeling, emotion, but also
imagination, intuition, memory, inspiration and so on.

In an essay, "Betrayal," James Hillman points out that as
the drama of Christ's betrayal unfolds:

> . . . the feminine becomes more and more appar-
> ent . . . the washing of the feet at the supper and
> the commandment to love; to the kiss and the
> silver; to the agony of Gethsemane—a garden, at
> night, the cup and the salty sweat pouring like
> drops of blood; to the wounded ear, to the image
> of the barren woman on the way to Golgotha; to
> the warning from the dream of Pilate's wife . . .
> to the wound in the side at the helpless moment
> of death, as Eve was torn from Adam's side. And
> finally, the discovery of the risen Christ, in white,
> by women.

In all the gospels it is women or a woman who first see
the resurrected Christ. As Reynolds Price says in his
Three Gospels:

> All the gospels admit a fact detrimental to their
> case in first-century Palestine—the empty tomb
> was discovered by women, women being thought
> unreliable witnesses. But where the other gospels
> mention small groups of women, John tells us
> only that Mary the Magdalene comes to the tomb
> early, while it is still dark; and finding the stone
> removed from the door, she runs to tell Peter and
> the Beloved (it is worth noting that, in her telling,
> the Magdalene may imply other companions in her
> visit—"we don't know where they have put him").

What this might mean is that it is through and by exploration and embrace of our feelings that we are most likely to first witness and experience the resurrection of our hearts, the miraculous renewal of hope, joy, liberty, eros, compassion, love. To the degree that we cherish, that is, give time and energy through attention, thought, and conversation, through the arts or therapy, and identify with these functions the Christ within us, the divinity in our natures becomes more visible and meaningful in our lives.

It also occurs to me that in the Parable of Cana, which is one of my favorite stories, in that I like to say that I believe in a Christ who brought wine to the party, it is Mary, the Mother of God, and in Catholic theology, the principle of mediation and matter, who first notices the need of the others, that is, the fact that the wine has run out, which observation she then shares with her Son.

In my faith, both religious and psychological, it is identification with the feminine aspect of our natures, *esse in anima*, feelings and intuition, that provides the most reliable and rewarding road toward the self-discovery that reveals just what our true and most basic needs really are.

For me then, as the poet William Everson in "Annul in Me My Manhood" writes in ecstatic, rhapsodic, agonized response:

> Make me then Girl-hearted, virgin-souled,
> woman-docile, maiden-meek; Cancel in me the
> rude compulsive tide that like an angry river
> surges through.

What *might* be returning through the vehicle of von Balthasar and Greeley, through the exquisite and copious refinements of the scholarly and theological imagination, and through the earthy humanity of Greeley's fiction— Greeley wrote dozens of novels each expressive of the kind of faith I am evoking here, and, now, through the New World papacy of Pope Francis, returning into and through the very heart of the Catholic Faith—is a form more reminiscent of the old Medieval Church.

The Medieval Church was a Church of miracles, mystery play and Marian devotion and a sense of a world steeped in Mary's presence. It was a Church of prayer and pilgrimage, of relics and rituals, of county fairs and sacred processions, a Church with a frank sensuality and bawdy sexuality, a Church of saints and feast days, of Christmas and May Day, and as Robert Graves writes:

> Christmas was merry in the middle ages, but May Day was merrier. It was the time of the beribboned Maypoles, of Collyridian cakes and ale, of wreaths and posies, of lovers' gifts, of archery contests, of merritotters (seesaws) and merribowks (great vats of milk punch). But particularly of mad-merry marriages, under the greenwood tree, when the dancers from the Green went off, hand in hand, into the greenwood and built themselves little love bowers and listened hopefully for the merry nightingale.

As Graves, hardly a Catholic sympathizer, makes clear, the Medieval Church was a Church of continuity and easy assimilation of order, often pagan rites and traditions. It was a Church with a deeply sacramental vision, that is, it believed that the Divine was manifest in the events, persons, places and things of ordinary living.

It was a Church whose spires stormed heaven, whose philosophy was brilliant, whose theology shone glory; and whose rational defense of a universal and intelligible nature prepared the way for modern science, whose legitimate development the Church is sometimes said to have opposed. As even Whitehead acknowledges, " . . . the faith in the possibility of science, generated antecedently to the development of modern scientific theory, is an unconscious derivative from medieval theology."

And, finally, through its sacramentalization of the order of chivalry, the Medieval Church restrained and chastened the violence of human nature, while converting its strength, not only into a force for good, but also a shield for the weak, which distinguishes Western chivalry from its counterparts in the East (Bushido). One of my favorite images in all of literature is Dante's image of the souls of Christian Warriors rising from the battlefield like sparks flying from a soothsayer's log.

Now, of course I recognize that I am over-idealizing here, but that's the romantic's way, many of whom looked back with great nostalgia to the unities of the Middle Ages, and the way of late nineteenth and early twentieth century writers I admire, such as Ruskin and Morris, Belloc and Chesterton.

A Medieval Christian. Catholics sometimes identify themselves through identification with a rite of Council in the Church, as in Tridentine or Vatican II Catholics.

My favorite of these is the way the great political philosopher Eric Voegelin described his status as being that
of a pre-Reformation Catholic. I suppose that's what I
am too. A pre-Reformation Catholic. A Medieval Catholic
who hopes that Morris and Scott, Chesterton, Belloc and
Graves were at least partially right.

A Celtic Christmas. A Medieval Catholic. This is my
fundamental orientation towards reality, as the existentialists say. Neither an orthodoxy or institution, my
Medieval Catholicism is an attitude, an "image"—"the
half-read wisdom of daemonic images, / Suffice the
aging man as once the growing boy" in which a deep
and local attachment to the persons, places and things
that I have known and loved, a fascination with Celtic
history, poetry and myth, Catholic theology, liturgy and
culture, together with certain romantic assumptions
about the meaning of life combine to create my "subjective equation"—my individual identity as a counselor
and as man.

Hugh MacDiarmid wrote a poem called "The Kind of
Poetry I Want." The kind of counseling I want is counseling with a Southern sense of place and pride and
courtesy, the moon and magnolia excess of its pulpit and
podium and stump speech language. I want the culture,
the Church-going, the cooking, and the cemeteries from
whence the dead keep close and constant watch upon the
living. I want the feel of swimming naked in a clear running creek in moonlight, the current slippery and cool,
bullfrogs croaking, a whippoorwill calling in the distance,
a billion stars up above in a slate blue summer's hazy
sky. I want Celtic poetry, passion and mysticism, the

earthy humor and frank ambition of Maeve, Cuchulian, Conchobar, Fergus, Ferdia, the supernaturalism of Finn. I want the memory of the famine and the great Irish Diaspora, Ellis Island, "my grandfather's immigrant eyes," as Guy Clark sings about them. I want the red hair, green eyes, and milk white skin of voluptuous Irish beauty. I want the moody but usually sprightly geniality of neighborhood bars, the boisterous, free-wheeling talk. I want folk tales and folk charms, front porch wisdom and back porch calm. I want the savvy of the Irish cop on the beat, the common sense and prudence of women keeping a family afloat with the money tight and a husband who gambles and drinks away his paycheck before he gets home. "The music of Scotland and Ireland" that Sorley MacLean remembers. I want the rawness and elemental sweep and surge of the later Yeats, Van Morrison's blues wail and troubadour lyricism, and I want the Catholic, the Medieval Catholic, ancient love of beauty and ritual, the rainbow-colored vestments of the priests, the candles, incense, and tinkling bells, its intellectual tradition, its theology, philosophy, epistemology, the flash frame luminosity of a syllogism-driven insight, the saints' days and feasts, the dignity and eternal truth of its teachings and traditions.

Finally, I am a romantic about counseling—

I'm a romantic about counseling because I know what it's meant in my own life.

May I tell you about my experience, not as a counselor but as a counselee?

It was during the early stages of the breakup of my first marriage, which had been a teenage marriage into which my wife and I had entered impulsively and which we had rather mechanically lived, that is to say, we both played out the roles we thought were expected of us.

My wife thought she was getting a young romantic burning with zeal, ambition, and philosophy, but what she got was my internalized image of my father, which meant that I pull my weight in the day, that I hold down a job and excel academically, come home in the evening, eat dinner, sit in my chair, read, watch TV, then fall asleep.

Need I say that there was a whole lot more to my father, though not much more to me at the time?

Anyway, we broke up. We sought counseling, after separating, with a pastor, not from our Church, but who was well known in the community as a gifted counselor, especially for young couples.

I went for a few sessions; the marriage was already irretrievably undermined by the weight of irreconcilable differences. But those sessions live in my memory—the counselor's gentleness and humanity.

We met in a park, Lee Park it's called, which a few years prior to our sessions, had been the gathering place for our local version of the Woodstock Nation, where I'd spent a lot of time. The park was overrun by early June greenness, the grounds not yet needing constant tending to escape being baked into cracks and dust by the summer heat. We met early in the morning, fluttering shadows from the trees as the slight breeze rustled, falling across the picnic table where we sat across from one another and talked.

He really did help me immensely. He did so in several ways and at several levels. There was just his presence—calm, unsurprised by successive bitter accusations of my wife, excuses for my own behavior, a few confessions of lingering doubt—and supportive of the mix of emotions that accompanied them. Without really saying very much, other than a gentle encouragement to continue, he helped me into awareness of my hornet's nest of anger, a hollow void of fear and loneliness, that before our session I would not have been able to identify, much less address.

But he didn't just listen. After encouraging me to talk for a time and through his nods and expression and occasional glance up at the trees nudging the conversation along in certain directions, he talked about himself. He talked about himself a lot. Mainly it was information that reassured me about the meaning and normality of what I had experienced, and what I would probably experience in the aftermath of the divorce. He talked to me about statistics relating to teenage marriages, the stages of grief that he observed, the risk of jumping into another relationship, etc.

He also asked me to do several things, some as simple as get some sleep and not to smoke so much—I chain-smoked the whole time we were together. He asked me what I had learned, if anything, from my marriage, about

me, about relationships, about life and my relationship
with God, and then, prescribed what in retrospect I would
have to call a ritual which involved gathering some
things that I wanted to preserve from the last five years
and depositing them in some special place where I could
find them again if I wanted.

That was more or less it. I met with him a few more times,
once in his Church office. My wife met with him as well.

Now if the goal of these sessions was to help us remain
together, they failed. If the goal was to help us manage
the separation and be responsible parents to our daugh-
ter, they failed even more grievously.

But I don't think these sessions failed to reach me—
reach me in a way that was immeasurable and inex-
pressible, at least in a way that would easily make sense
to anyone else. I think these sessions gave me hope, a
better feeling about myself, a better sense of what those
feelings were. Self-understanding and self-acceptance
would be the relevant shrink terms. And I also got something that I could do that didn't quite make sense to me,
but had an impact nevertheless.

I sought out therapy to be heard and accepted, and I
wanted to do something or be told what to do so that I
could both feel, get, and do better. From this counselor I
received guidance.

I would add as both a further confession and caution-
ary tale that I underwent for a very brief interval, six
months, a classical Jungian analysis, from which I

dropped out for what at the time seemed persuasive reasons, but ones that proved eventually to be little more than rationalizations. The truth was that although already a graduate student, married, with a child, I'd never separated from my family of origin, and was terrified as well of facing my own inner sadness, despair and depression. With a great deal of sensitivity and understanding, my analyst tried to dissuade me, but I, in the textbook sense, was resistant. Within six months I was in the grip of the worst depression of my life, laid low, and virtually nonfunctional, drifting through my days with all the energy and direction of leaves along the highway, blown and shifted by the movement of passing cars.

And yet, despite my abortive termination, when I think about my time in analysis—the dream work and amplifications, with analyst and analysand guzzling coffee from an instant coffee maker, in the background the blue-green tranquil glow and hypnotic sound of the large aquarium that the analyst kept in his office—an unanticipated peace and calm steals over my soul.

Something "took" I suppose, though it took me a long time to acknowledge it.

I'm a counselor. I distrust any word more pretentious than that. Counselor really is a noble word with a noble lineage. You'll find it in Shakespeare. You won't find analyst or psychiatrist or psychologist.

I also like the term psychotherapy mainly because it's pretentious enough to be generic, in that psychiatrists don't usually think it is beneath them, and it's unregulated, which means its use and definition is not in the hands of legislators, bureaucrats, and academics.

I believe in counseling. I believe in psychotherapy. I've witnessed the transformations it can bring. I've seen the soul open like a fragile flower, flushed with dawn, reaching for the sun, after being hurt, abused, hopeless, waterless, wounded, deserted, stunted, trampled in the dust. I believe in counseling, believe it can change lives, lift hearts, inspire spiritual growth, believe it can work. It must work on one level quite practically and solidly, to make ordinary day-to-day life more satisfying and less problem-filled, less anxiety-ridden, more adaptive and functional, strengthening the observing ego, as the Freudians say, or common sense, which would be the Adlerian equivalent, but it must also, on another more meaningful level, work to reinvigorate spiritual, sexual, and vocational passion, stir courage, enhance pleasure, renew love, maximize fun, create joy, add rhythm and music to the day, serenity to the evening, depth to sleep, freshness to labor, spirit to religion, soul rejoined to heart, so that with the old Celtic prayer the soul itself can say:

> I am a flame of fire, blazing with passionate love;
> I am a spark of light, illuminating the deepest
> truth; I am a rough ocean, heaving with righteous
> anger; I am a calm lake, comforting the troubled
> beast; I am a wild storm raging at human sins; I
> am a gentle breeze blowing hope in the troubled
> heart; I am dry dust, choking worldly ambition; I
> am wet earth bearing rich fruits of grace.

I'm a counselor. It's how I make my living and how I
spend my days, all day, except with luck, to steal away
a few minutes to prepare speeches, "soul-fire sermons"
such as this book.

I think as a counselor that I've been privileged to learn
two things about human life that probably otherwise
would have escaped me, or at best, about them I would
have felt more unsure.

The first is that as a consequence of my experience I
know—I don't just believe, I know—that inside of every
human being, no matter how bitter, angry, criminal,
abused or traumatized, there is a larger Self struggling to
be born and breathe. Call this larger Self, the Spirit, the
Soul, the Higher Self, the spark of divinity, the Christ or
the Buddha or the Atman within us—call it whatever you
want, but it's there.

Second, I know that what most of us see, or think we
see, about the truth of other's people's lives, is not, once
the inessentials are stripped away and all pretense overcome, what really pulses. Other people are not happier,
not better, not different because of their skin or religion
or culture, not more stable, more content; instead, we're
all more or less the same. And that identity, as we live it,
is something very far removed from what the moralists,
the advertisers, the experts, columnists and editorialists,
and of course, above all, the politicians, pretend it is. It's
very alien to the iconography and public orthodoxy and
definitions of what is "normal," and these assumptions
about "what everybody knows," of what "they or the
neighbors will think," into which we all are socialized, or

in terms of which we are, in a very literal sense, brain-washed, become the means by which we become alienated from ourselves, so that for fear of being viewed as crazy, abnormal, alien, we lose touch with the voices and angels of our deepest truth and conscience.

When I was younger, each morning when I got the newspaper I used to read the front page and editorials before anything else, if I stooped to read anything else. Now, with decades of experience as a counselor, I turn first to the sports, the horoscope and the comics. They're much more truthful and reliable in their revelations of human nature.

What I have been laboring here to do, in this first chapter, is to tell you about my heart and soul; my "story" or "narrative"; the loyalties and loves that motivate me; my deepest wish, perhaps a childhood wish born from watching Disney, my wish upon a star; the deepest part of me; the Higher Self that I've just talked about. Another name for this is identity. One of the best descriptions of identity that I've ever run across is found in a book by Andres Rodriguez, *The Book of the Heart: The Poetics, Letters, and Life of John Keats,* where he writes:

> I know from Keats that the intensity and form of identity is intrinsic, that is, essential to life, beyond one's origin in any particular class or race, and it is absolutely tied to vocation. Yet all the details of life (Cockney English, Mexican American, working class, and so on) are also what anyone has to work with, and one must not despair that there is ultimately no comprehensive expression of identity, because there is. It's what a very wise

friend of mine calls *el son entero*. An inner music or spiritual song.

Now I think that counseling, whether experienced as a counselee, or a counselor who practices his art, his vocation, his counseling as a spiritual discipline, a means of developing character and reason with understanding, can be the means, the midwifery, to use the old Socratic metaphor, for the birth and growth, the formation and education of this Higher Self.

It's fundamentally what my counseling is all about. I'm very much attracted to the phrase *soul-making*, which Keats first used and Hillman has made the motto of his archetypal psychology. But that's Keats's phrase and Hillman's psychology. I think my own orientation is much more religious in the conventional sense.

So that is what I've been singing, doing, making, soul-making—singing a spiritual song of myself, a spiritual existentialist song, evoking my identity as a counselor and a human being, one filled with the spirit, with yearning and longing, an ache for transcendence, beauty, unity, and wholeness, but one firmly anchored in what Pound called the "phalanx of particulars" of my own life, history, region, language, culture, ethnicity, and religion.

A spiritual existentialist Self—to midwife its birth, to further its growth and joy, its formation and evolution—that's the aim of spiritual existentialist psychology and counseling.

CHAPTER TWO

HEALING COUNSELING'S THOUGHT AND SPEECH DISORDER

In after years, the friends of Jackson wrested with the problem of what gave his judgment a specific gravity — "The character of his mind," remarked Benton, "was that of judgment, with a rapid and almost intuitive perception, followed by an instant and decisive action." "General Jackson is the most rapid reasoner I ever met with," declared Louis McLane. "He jumps to a conclusion before I can start on my premises." "He was indeed an extraordinary man," wrote the author James Kirke Paulding, "the only man I ever saw that excited my admiration to the pitch of wonder. To him knowledge seemed entirely unnecessary. He saw intuitively into everything, and reached a conclusion by a short cut, while others were beating the bush for game."

—Arthur M. Schlesinger, Jr., *The Age of Jackson*

Churchill's feeling for the English tongue was sensual, almost erotic; when he coined a phrase he would suck it, rolling it around his palate to extract its full flavor. On first meeting Violet Asquith he told her that words had "a magic and music" all their own.

—William Manchester, *The Last Lion: Winston Spencer Churchill, Visions of Glory 1874–1932*

If the birth and formation of a spiritual existentialist self is a legitimate goal for counseling, the prize upon which we as counselors ought to keep our eyes, then I think to fulfill or reach it will require two fundamental shifts away from what now is considered normative.

The first is that as counselors attempting to create "models" and develop "theories," we must try more to "think" in the way that we "think" while counseling, while we're with a client trying to figure out what's going on and how to do something valuable that helps; and, second we must struggle to "talk," that is write in our journals, and present in our workshops and symposia, about these concerns the way we talk in counseling, the way I'm trying to address you, the reader, now as if you were sitting across from me hoping for help, *with* whatever healing and truth I can bring.

Both of these notions are derived from the work of James Hillman. Throughout his twenty-some-odd books, but especially *The Myth of Analysis*, where an entire section is devoted to "psychological language," Hillman has crafted and modeled a way of thinking about psychotherapy consistent with the way we think in psychotherapy. At various places he gives it various names, but most typically, it's "being psychological." And in *A Hundred Years of Psychotherapy—And the World is Getting Worse*, he says succinctly, "We must begin to talk about psychotherapy the way we talk in psychotherapy."

So what is that thought and speaking like? How, as counselors, do we think—when we're in a session, supervising, participating in a team behind a one-way mirror?

The thought—would you disagree?—is speculative, probing, practical, concrete, engaged, exploratory, intuitive, descriptive, anecdotal, phenomenological, a-linear, non-discursive, discontinuous, disorderly, advancing in an energetic spiraling meander, like children playing hide and seek as they walk home from school while taking as long as they can to do it.

In my view, the most defining feature of thought that heals, or can even hope to heal, is that it is emotional, soaked with the sap and sensitivity of feeling, the force that through the green fuse drives and has the tenderness of new grown leaves.

It's on your toes, fly-by-the-seat-of-your-pants, and not as the crow flies, but as the swan flies circling and circling above the lake, a white speck against a firmament of blue, then a gentle graceful dive to settle on the crystal bright waters.

It's not abstract, systematic, or logical. It's involved and concrete. It's passionate and poetic. In classical epistemology it would be described as belonging to the field of practical, rather than speculative, wisdom.

A tradition sustains this. What I've described as "thinking about counseling as we think in counseling" is representative of a mode of thought recognized to be a powerful tool of both self-exploration and the comprehension of truth. It's not just touchy-feely thought, loaded with adjectives, overstrained caprice. It is romantic thought, which originates with feeling, or as Coleridge said, "deep thinking is attainable only by a man of deep feeling," but culminates with the disciplined insights of genuine thought. Again, Coleridge, "feelings die by flowing into the mold of intellect, becoming ideas." Or Wordsworth who felt that significant art can be attained only "by a man who, being possessed of more than usual organic sensibility, has also thought long and deeply. For our continued influxes of feeling are modified and directed by our thoughts, which are indeed the representatives of all our past feelings."

The literary critic Harold Bloom believes that when considered in the context of the literary tradition the defining feature of romanticism is its "internalization of the quest romance." ("The Internalization of the Quest Romance" in *Romanticism and Criticism*, ed. Harold Bloom, New York: Norton, 1970). Prior to the Romantics, the quest romance was an "actual" event, occurring in objective time and space that inspired the poet's praise and narrative. But with the Romantics, the quest becomes a "subjective" event in subjectively experienced time and space. Whether in Wordsworth himself, or in Wordsworthian-type meditations by the other great High Romantic poets, the quester "traveled" through the field of his own experience, especially in its most commonplace and ordinary forms, in search of truth and beauty. In this sense, Romanticism foreshadows, or more accurately said, initiates the phenomenological existentialist project, for the phenomenologist, too, is a sort of "quester" who risks engagement with his own portion of ordinary experience in a deliberate encounter that he hopes will be luminous and expressive of meaning. So this mode of thought is not only romantic, it is also eminently phenomenological.

And it is also "psychological."

What drawing on Hillman's work I am calling "counseling thought," Hillman himself calls "being psychological" and personifies as knight-errantry. He writes:

> The Knight Errant is a wanderer, and his path has been deviant ever since Parmenides descried loose-limbed wandering as the way of error, deceptive opinion, going astray. For the grand rational tradition, the way of psychologizing, is

too close to *phantasia* and the *senses*, having
wandered off course and away from the true logos
of intellectual reasoning, intuitional revelation,
and the eternalities of spirit. The Knight Errant
follows fantasy, riding the vehicle of his emotions;
he loiters . . . regarding desire as also holy; and he
listens to the deviant discourse of the imagination.

To think about counseling the way we think in counseling is, then, to think romantically, phenomenologically,
existentially, to be always "underway" as Heidegger
says, on the road, Hillman's Knight Errant.

Further, this way of thinking about counseling bends
back upon the counseling process itself which we can
now see more clearly as a "romance," a spiritual, spiraling, jousting, mysterious, erotic passage through ordinary
experience in quest of beauty and meaning. And the vehicle for this adventure, the spirited mount, the war horse
or *destrier,* whether humbly harnessed, or shod and ca-
parisoned in silver, scarlet, and gold, is talk—the talking
cure. Talk, dialogue, beautiful and useful conversation.

Therapeutic speech that expresses therapeutic talk, that
is, talking about counseling the way we talk in counseling, is maybe even a bit more random and hyperbolic.

As I said in my introduction, it longs to set Church
bells ringing in the heart. But, as I try to think and talk
about suffering or sex or power as we think and talk in
counseling, with someone who is struggling with these
issues, there is something missing, a one-on-one relationship. The old Jungian way, I once heard, was knee to
knee, in absolute renunciation of the detachment of the

couch. Talk in psychotherapy occurs within a personal
relationship, at its best maybe even the existentialists
call the "I-thou" relationship. What a strange relationship it is. Counselor and client—you're companions who
are glad to see each other, who relieve each other's loneliness; you're colleagues in a mutual work of recreating a
narrative, a story, a life so that it can become more fulfill-
ing; it's an erotic connection: you get into each other's
fantasies and dreams; it's a relationship determined by
respect for each other's need, wonder at each other's
presence; it includes transference and counter-transfer-
ence, perhaps, the transfer and reenactment of feelings
more properly belonging to prior loves and relationships;
it's a power struggle for whose in charge; it's an economic relationship where the client is both customer who
pays the bills and boss who can fire you at any time;
it's teacher-study, preacher and preached to; it's confes-
sor and confessed, parent and child, lover and beloved,
performer and observer, exhibitionist and voyeur, actor
and audience, the dancer and the danced; and probably a
thousand other things as well.

But gladly, as with counseling thought, there is a tradition for this, a tradition of writing that is geared toward a
personal connection to the reader. Hillman calls it psychological speech—

> Psychological remembrance is given by the kind
> of speech that carries remembrance within it.
> This language is both of culture and uncultured,
> is both of art and artless. It is mythic, metaphoric
> language, a speech of ambiguities that is evoca-
> tive and detailed, yet not definitive, not produc-
> tive of dictionaries, textbook, or even abstract

descriptions. Rather it is a speech that leads to participation, in the Platonic sense, in and with the thing spoken of, a speech of stories and insights which evoke, in the other who listens, new stories and new insights, the way one poem and one tune ignite another verse and song. It is conversation, letters, tales, in which we reveal our dreams and fantasies. It evokes, calls forth, and creates psyche as it speaks. It speaks of mood: of "sadness" and "despair" before depression; of "rage" before aggression; of "fear," "panic" and "anguish" before anxiety attacks.

Hillman goes on to quote Tertullian, but being a bit less heterodox I choose St. Bernard—

St. Bernard habitually writes artistic, rhythmical prose; at times, overcome with intense enthusiasm and great spiritual ardor, he will sing a hymn or a doxology similar to those found in the epistles of St. Paul or the confessions of St. Augustine. When he writes—for he is essentially a writer, and in this sense a man of letters—he always writes for someone, he is always addressing someone, and it is just as if he were speaking. His talent for oratory is given free rein. In any literary work, he remains an orator, and to be more precise, a Christian orator. He is a preacher and he needs an audience. He needs to express himself in order to find an outlet for his inner fervor, he has to communicate his love, and in expressing it, he feels it more intensely. His style is always oratorical, but especially when he composes sermons. Bernard never thinks of his audience in the abstract . . . But Bernard is

a universal doctor because of the fact that he is
an orator; his message, though addressed to all,
still retains its personal quality. He is a man with
a human heart who thinks, prays, suffers, and
yearns . . . In his letters and treatises as well as
his sermons, his written style remains an oral one
because Bernard cannot cease being an orator.
(Jean Leclercq, *The Love of Learning and the Desire for
God*, p. 218.)

Perhaps now we can double back on the counseling
conversation—now when I say conversation I don't mean
at all the garden-variety low-key, laid-back, Beckett-
like, flat-affect exchange of trivia and hollow courtesies
that we often call "conversation"; no, I'm hearkening
back to the times when the only kinds of stars were the
ones up in the sky, before the global infantilization and
homogenization caused by the omnipresence of media
that allow most of us to get our social needs and needs
for stimulation met through a passive soaking up of a
barrage of round-the-clock available stimuli—and, no I
don't think fidgeting with a mouse and being able to type
back instantly a message makes much difference—a time
when human conversation was the chief attraction of the
day, the main source for social stimulation, so naturally
expanded its range to accommodate every human concern and emotion.

But anyways, perhaps we can double back to the therapeutic stimulation and eliminate those tendencies, to
which most of us regularly yield, to sound to our clients
the same way our teachers and mentors sound to us
through the medium of the professional literature—in
other words, the tendency to sound pretty boring, pom-

pous, and abstract, while we're thinking that we're simply speaking in a professional manner.

One specific technique might be what Lynn Hoffman calls "situating" one's ideas. She writes:

> Another deconstructive practice would be the habit of "situating" one's professional knowledge. I will sometimes pull a suggestion or interpretation out of the bag I have labeled "Biggest Hits of Family Therapy," but I try to include the story of how I came by it and how it is supposed to work.
> (Lynn Hoffman, "Postmodernism in Family Therapy," *The Evolution of Psychotherapy*, p. 346. See Bibliography for complete reference.)

Hoffman calls this kind of sharing with the client "deconstructive." I would call it existentialist, in that it was existentialism that first reminded us of the "situatedness" or "historicity" of human knowledge. Existentialism emphasizes the "perspectival" nature of all truth, not its ultimate relativity, which is the deconstructive argument. I would also call sharing with the client the origins, history, source, and previous experience with any idea or intervention that you might be proposing, a spiritual virtue, since admitting to a client that you're human and fallible requires humility, which is a spiritual virtue.

But whether it be "deconstructivist," "existentialist," or "spiritual," the idea to share with a client just exactly why one is suggesting something and where the idea came from in the first place is a good one. And it's an equally good idea to think that a major advance in counseling technique would be the elimination of language or attitude on the part of the counselor that insists upon or implies any kind of superiority or privilege or any greater claim on truth of scientific over anecdotal, research over clinical, empirical over speculative, professional over human, "situated" knowledge or discourse.

We should think and talk about counseling the way we think and talk in counseling, and then we ought to readjust technique and language in counseling to what is naturally presented there.

And as I'm sure you know, and perhaps tire of by now, the way I connect to this tradition of rhetoric, or psychological speech, of talking about counseling the way we talk in counseling is through my Southern-souled identity, through the South, through the Southern love for oral tradition, for stump-speaking, stem-winding eloquence. The South. The South, Southern culture, Delta cotton, moonshine, moonlight, sweating all day in the Church pews, cornbread, iced tea, fishing all Sunday afternoon, deer horn, hunting dogs baying, front-porch-swinging hybrid of ancient Gaelic and African culture.

And the preachers! The preachers! As Camille Paglia admits:

> Flicking the radio dial in America, one hears bursts of beautiful, spellbinding poetry. But it is neither academics nor contemporary writers who are filling the air with dazzling imagery and profound spiritual truths. Alas for progressive politics, these are the voices of white and black, reading from the Bible.

It's a rhapsodizing, intemperate, high-galloping language, spiced with the lyrical interlude, this *hwyll* of the sonorous psalmist, this sexual-spiritual dream-like synthesis, this holy-rolling, rock-and-rolling rhythm.

There's a Gaelic connection too. One reason I write is because it keeps me honest as a counselor, betters my art. While I'm writing my ears are perked up in sessions a little, so that in this sense this is a kind of work song, a song that I sing in the fields, my field of counseling perhaps—and certainly in its flamboyance and mixing of metaphors and abrupt shifts of imagery—perhaps, like the woman's work songs sung by Gaelic women in the fields, about which one scholar has written:

> At the other end of the poetic spectrum we find the Dionysian poetry that has survived largely in songs used to accompany various forms of communal labor . . . Their poetry unfolds, not in a smooth linear movement, but unevenly, with quite unpredictable changes in focus. But however disconcerting this may at times be, it is precisely these abrupt transitions from image to image, governed only by the nature of the situation expressed in the poem, that release the creative energy. These songs use language according to a principle which is the furthest extreme from that of the logical, ordered sequences in prose. Out of the kaleidoscope of images, fusing and separating in oral transmission, certain more permanent forms were from time to time created . . . These tender, intensely passionate songs with their elemental themes provide the main lyrical impulse

of Gaelic poetry. (John MacInnes, *The Gaelic Continuum in Scotland*, p. 277.)

Southern and Celtic—that's my way. But I would also encourage you to make your own trip home. When you go deep into any tradition you are likely to find a music there, the rhythm and poetry of your heart. You'll find your language, the song of yourself, your soul. You'll find a way to move deeper into the counseling event and relationship. You'll find a deeper way to heal. In part this trip is ethnic, cultural, racial, but I encourage you to make it a religious pilgrimage too. The music that exists in the heart and soul of culture can get you drunk, can make you fog your eyes and blur your senses so that the recovery and repossession of one's soul song, one's identity and language can separate rather than connect. One can begin to feel a certain distance and alienation from the "Other," the "Stranger," from those unlike you. But religion can temper and ultimately transform this because all the major religious traditions are ultimately universalist in aspiration; all religions greet all humanity as one community under God. The only time in my life when I have ever experienced a community where the differences of race, ethnicity, culture, and history were simply overcome in the sense that diversity truly was exclusively a source of joy and humor, good stories, good talk, a learning experience rooted in friendship and love, was one night eating dinner in a Catholic rectory in the company of eight priests—a Cajun, a Chicago Irish, a Texas hill country Anglo, a Nigerian, a Filipino, a Korean, a San Salvadorean, a Mexican-American Tex-Mex, and me.

So make that pilgrimage, but keep your eyes lifted up to the hills.

But there is still another cipher. The voice. My voice. I'm a voice junkie. A voice mystic. I became one as a boy listening to the oratory of the South, from pulpit and podium, from preacher to politician. And I became one forever the first time I heard Dylan Thomas read, read on one of those Cadmus tapes, read "A Child's Christmas in Wales" or "Fern Hill."

The voice—"My voice shall go with you," said Erickson, and said a client from a week ago in answer to "Why did you stop at that moment?" "I heard your voice," he said.

Erickson is the great transitional figure here. But, unfortunately Milton Erickson was no Anton Mesmer. Unlike his great nineteenth-century precursor, Erickson was not a romantic philosopher. He didn't create a philosophy equal to his own charisma and gifts.

The voice.

The voice concentrates power.

It sighs with love.

It sings with soul.

It can do what an experienced hand can do to a lover's body.

It can send shivers up and down your spine.

Make you feel like you want to fly.

Thrill you, hurt you, excite you.

It can tickle you, make you throb, bring goose bumps to your flesh—

The voice of Ella Fitzgerald, Frank Sinatra, Muddy Waters, John Lee Hooker, Van Morrison, John Fogerty, Johnny Cash.

The voice of Dylan Thomas, Richard Burton, Orson Welles, James Earle Jones, Sean Connery, Barbara Jordan, Maya Angelou.

And the best of all voices, The Lord of the Voice, Hoyt Axton—if you don't recognize the name, get the video *The Black Stallion*, a truly magical tale, spellbinding to both adults and kids—he narrates that—narrates, with a down-home flavor, a gambler's winnings on his lap, to the wide-eyed smiling wonder of his son, the tale of Alexander and the fiery steed Bucephalous. It's a quintessential Southern voice—the voice of red wine in a paper cup, wild hog in the barbecue pit being slowly lacquered with hickory and wild mint and onion-flavored sauce, folks out on the lawn, lanterns hung from the trees, the sky blushed red and glowing on the horizon, the scent of honeysuckle on the breeze.

The voice of the counselor, to anticipate—like the voice of the bard? Or a preacher? Or a rock musician accompanied by musical instrument, whose chant "flows effort-lessly from the mouth." Words were honey, dew on the tongue, soothing ointments that fall like snowflakes or bloom like wildflowers after a soft summer rain. As Eric Havelock, the great classicist says, "the poetic utterance is identified as though it were a thing in itself and flows like a river."

And like the voice of a preacher, certainly.

Counselor as bard, poet, preacher, rock and roller, holy roller, talker, talking your ear off—impregnating through the ear.

The voice is truly at the heart of what we do as counselors. It can and ought to be played like an instrument, the wail of the pipes, the crystalline flow and vibration and thrum of the harp or the wail of the sax or the whiskey-warm hum of the harmonica.

To truly speak about counseling as we speak in counseling we must find a way to sound out our souls and selves, to integrate the voice into our "professional" language. Sound out. Sound off. *Sounder*—do you remember that movie?

What I'll do in the next chapter, is try to develop an Anton Mesmer-like philosophy, in terms of spiritual existentialism, to mesmerize you, to think about and talk about a theory of counseling, a theory of what and how clients change through counseling, a theory of personality and neurosis, and, then fair warning: a head 'em up, move 'em out, thunder-knocking-at-the-door, rebel-rousing-yell political statement—and I'll indicate why I think that necessary.

I call them theories. What they really are, are rules of thumb.

They are "thickenings" that attempt to stay in the "thick of" the natural articulations, contours, and shapes already implicitly configuring the counseling experience. This was the Way of Phenomenology as practiced by the French philosopher Maurice Merleau-Ponty.

As I detail them, let me be clear, I do not suppose myself to be presenting a verifiable hypothesis. These are ad hoc ideas—Rules of Thumb, as I said, that are intended to be a means for getting a grip on a problem, and be gripped by it, a way to take or get a pulse, to probe for pressure points or find new pleasure spots. I am presenting a "theory" in the ancient sense of "theoria," the Greek from which our word derives, which described a tale told to his friends by a traveler who had returned from a visit to some distant site.

Anything beyond a flexible rule of thumb theory hampers whatever grace or ability I might have as a counselor. It limits my "availability," my ability to keep my head in the game so to speak, my concentration focused. There are some athletes who just get out there and play. There are some who are students of the game but in large part just play, generally aware of a certain game plan or strategy that they might have, but making most moves on the basis of instinct and intuition. And there are still others able to visualize a game as a chalkboard diagram of x's and o's, geometry and angles, and then go out and execute their game plan, seeing every play, every move as an instancing, rough or smooth, of the perfect play or game plan that they continually polish. This last group really are the artists of the game, their natural language is aesthetic, they talk about elegance and symmetry.

As a counselor I'm very much in the second category. I devote time to ideas and theory, but whenever I've tried to keep my theory very much in mind, trying to create a perfect strategy or intervention, or analyzing a client's material or expressions according to an analytic theory of the mind, pretty soon I feel hog-tied and strain to break loose. I end up doing something just because "it occurred to me to say or do it" and I have no other justification.

So let me wrap up this time on needed shifts in counseling, on thinking and speaking about counseling the way that we think and talk in counseling, by saying that I think these shifts are more than just a little underway.

First, there is Hillman, whose demand that we make these shifts, forming the themes of this chapter—the wonder of his work and example.

Unfortunately, it is hard to look to Hillman as a leader in counseling because after years of tossing Molotov cocktails into the consulting room, whose effects I would say were bracing, Hillman officially, and with fanfare at a world gathering of Jungians in Paris, quit practicing analysis. Although I was never analyzed by Hillman, my guess is that this was not exactly like Michael Jordan giving up basketball. The sheer volume of Hillman's work indicates that he didn't have a lot of time left over.

But gladly there was a Michael Jordan of psychotherapy. I mean Salvadore Minuchin, and Minuchin's thinking and talking about family therapy has undergone a progressive and accelerating transformation along the lines for which I've been calling. In a response to a paper by Minuchin, Jeffrey Zeig remarked: "Sal Minuchin is easy to categorize; he is cybernetician, a Zen rabbi, a sociodramatist, a humorist, and a strategist."

If twenty-five years ago you saw Minuchin in person or observed him in an actual family therapy session, you would have known this. But you wouldn't have known it if you read his books, which were as functionally prosaic as any mechanical how-to manual. But that changed, and changed dramatically, as Minuchin, experimenting with a variety of genres and styles, became an exceedingly compelling writer who sounds in his books as creative and confrontational, as wild and wooly and as weird as he did in person or in session.

Family therapy itself is moving along these lines. The language of the journals and conferences sounds different, is more adventurous and creative than it was ten years ago. Ten years ago sticks in my mind, because ten years ago I submitted my first and only paper to the journal *Family Process*, which was rejected, with very warm praise, on the grounds that "it was not the kind of paper that was published in *Family Process*."

The paper became the basis of my first book, *Adoption Charms and Rituals for Healing*, a crazy quilt, olla-podrida brew of Hillmanian-inspired vision, Ericksonian strategies and stories, all wrapped up in Celtic mysticism, romance, and poetry, a practical manual in spiritual existentialism. I think I would be succumbing only slightly to the famous Celtic propensity to boast, at which all the ancient Roman writers sniffed disapprovingly, to say that *Charms and Rituals* literally changed the field of adoption.

But speaking of adoption, I don't want to be overly optimistic. Years ago I became involved in a feud over the editorship of a proposed "academic" journal on adoption that grew out of a meeting between several of the "leaders" in the field. I thought that on the basis of my published work I deserved it. An academic rival thought he deserved it. The original planning group split over the issue. In a fiery exchange of insults, he accused me of wanting control because otherwise, I quote, "The kind of thing you write would not be accepted by a properly refereed journal." "Well, it has been," I wrote back, "and the first paper I submitted to a properly academic journal was described by its editor as 'the best written paper I've received in ten years.'" I also pointed out that the only way that he could put a book together was by hiring a journalist to assist him, which is precisely what he and a colleague had done.

Hiring a journalist to help you write a book—well, to me, that's like buying a crutch to help you walk; it may keep you upright, but it ain't got any melody or music, and it ain't gonna help you dance or sing.

As Yeats said (I think),

> We must laugh and we must sing
> We are blest by everything.

And then louder sing, louder sing—

> . . . for man is but a paltry thing, a tattered coat upon a stick
>
> Unless Soul clap its hands and sing, and louder sing for every tatter in its moral dress.

Laugh and sing and louder sing. Laugh and sing, and louder sing is what I hope we all can do, or at least do more of, in our professional prose, in our papers, with our clients, in our hearts and souls. Louder sing. Counseling with heart and soul. I do get touchy. I am a touchy-feely therapist.

CHAPTER THREE

⫴

THE TALKING CURE

The old general was a demanding parent-correspondent . . . Still more instruction followed a few weeks later: "I would . . . commend to your particular attention a poem of Burns'. It is his advice to a young friend, Andrews. In my course of life, I have found (it) one of the most salutary, as well as one of the safest guides that I have met with in life . . . Memorize it by all means, the beautiful emanation of heart, and intellect. I esteem it one of the riches & treasures of memory. Possess yourself of it, my Dear Boy; and act upon its teachings – through life, and you will never have cause of regret . . . I am glad that you received your Hat, and that it suits you."

—James L. Haley, *Sam Houston*

L et me begin with the Hunter Who Never Came Home From the Hill, a Scot, a Celt, of course: Robert Louis Stevenson, from his essay on "Talk and Talkers":

There can be no fairer ambition than to excel at talk . . . to have a fact, a thought, or an illustration, pat to every subject; and not only to cheer the flight of time among our intimates, but bear our part in that great international congress, always sitting, where public wrongs are first declared, public errors first corrected, and the course of public opinion shaped, day by day, a little nearer to the right . . . And it is in talk alone that we can learn our period and ourselves. In short, the first duty of a man is to speak; that is his chief business in this world and talk, which is the harmonious speech of two or more, is by far the most accessible of pleasures . . . it completes

our education, founds and fosters our friend-
ships, and can be enjoyed at any age and in
almost any state of health . . .

A good talk is not to be had for the asking.

This is as fine a description—an incantation, even—of
what eventuates in counseling, of what is called "process," as I have ever encountered. "The first duty of a
man is to speak" but, as Stevenson also says, "a good
talk is not to be had for the asking"; instead, it must be
inspired—"let's get started"; founded—"what shall we
talk about today?"; fostered—"go on, say more"; cultivated—"let's dig down into that," "let me address that,"
"let me talk about that a little"; pursued—"I think we
should explore that," "really go after it," "find out where
it leads." This is the art of the counselor—to be "prop
and pillar," as Faulkner said, to the human spirit's capacity to endure and prevail. We are all talk, no action, or,
rather, we're adepts and artisans at that most ennobling
and enlivening of all human actions: good conversation.

If we stay close to the bone, stick strictly to the given, go
back, as the phenomenologists say, "to the things themselves" precisely as they are given, then we must say
that counseling, before it is anything else, consists of a
conversation, a dialogue, talk, a talk, a "talking cure."
As Freud said, "Nothing takes place in a psychoanalytic
treatment but an interchange of words between the patient and the analyst." In counseling, two or more people
get together and talk with the assumption that this is
a special kind of talk in which one person, the client or
clients, assume that on the basis of the information that
he, she, or they provide, the other person, the counselor,

will say something that relieves their distress or solves their problem.

The client also may already believe, on the basis of what he or she "knows" through the verbal or written testimony of others, or may come to believe, either on the evidence of the experience of counseling or as a result of persuasion on the part of the counselor, that the counseling interchange itself, the to-and-fro, the ventilation, exploration, and dialogue itself provides relief and healing. In other words, the event of the dialogue, the heat and energy of it, generates new experiences, attitudes, and solutions of which neither counselee or counselor, alone, in the absence of the actual occurrence—conversation would have been capable. In the process truth may emerge and crystallize.

The "method" or "technique" of counseling is phenomenology, which may be more "phenomenologically" described as descriptive amplification.

The way I learned it was as a graduate student in phenomenological existential psychology. Our method of research was to select a phenomenon: love, anger, shame, hospitality, grief, etc.—for reasons which we understood to be "subjectively," not neutrally, determined—then gather blind protocols; that is, without explaining or predetermining more than would necessarily occur though our request for the description, we asked our "subjects" to write or speak into an audiotape machine of their experience of the phenomenon "in question." We'd then go over these descriptions again and again, attempting to abstract "meaning units" from which we would then develop a structural description of the "meaning" of the phenomena.

This method was an adaptation to psychology of the phenomenological philosopher Edmund Husserl's philosophical method of "free fantasy variation."

Over time, however, I moved in my method away from Husserl, and the residue of philosophical "idealism" that survives in his work. The idea of abstraction was dropped, to be replaced with a more Heideggerian and existentialist style of attempting to "illuminate" the meaning from the descriptions themselves in interplay with our presence and questioning. This took the form of a continuous repetitive engagement with the "material," not unlike, for instance, the way an actor studies a script trying to arrive at the essence of his character, going over and over it again, experimenting with different tones and emphases in terms of which—"in *terms* of which," a precise term in this context, truth happened. Provisionally, and perhaps poetically, given that truth and beauty in Heidegger, like Keats, are inseparable, we "risked"—another good Heideggerian term—"meaning."

This "meaning" or truth could then be elucidated and contextualized through historical, philosophical, and literary amplification in order to appreciate it in its density, wonder and reverberations.

Transferred to therapy, this quasi-Heideggerian method—though I would call it von Balthasarian in the sense that von Balthasar shared Heidegger's conception of "truth as revelation" necessarily joining beauty and meaning—means just talking it to death, to life, just going over the same ground again and again, going back to what you said last week, revisiting, changing, adding, enriching, altering, enlarging, editing, enlightening, educating, informing, teaching, releasing, touching, moving, stirring, inspiring. It's life lived, and counseling done in the foundational image, the archetypal motif of the Celtic spiral. And, this amplifying or illumining or spiraling through the process occurs in something like a meditative state, the mood of young lovers, the concentration of the athlete, the silence of the prayerful, the ecstasy of the dancer, the transport of the preacher storming through his ocean of words.

Perhaps the best way, from my point of view, to describe what actually happens in effective counseling, that is the changes that are wrought thereby, is through a continuous process of amplification or spiraling which in its interpersonal dimension becomes progressively co-creative and collaborative, but in which the counselor takes the initial lead, as occurs, for example, between partners in a dance, which may or may not include, in light of the lyric and beat of the movement:

• Identification, affirmation, and expression of feelings and desires that may have been unknown, ignored, or denied.

• Reality-testing—explanation and articulation of reasonable expectations, customs, norms, principles, information, and truths that are applicable.

• Skill acquisition through explanation, instruction or directives.

• Attachment and socialization primarily through the example and experience of the counselor-counselee relationship.

• Restructuring through identification, challenge, instruction and practice of the ideational process; reducing, as the cognitive-behavior folks say, of automatic thoughts, erroneous ideas, false beliefs, self-defeating assumptions, inconsistencies, over-generalizations, and analytically-defined defenses.

• Interpretations that may be true, or "more true," in the sense of "noble ascriptions" and "positive connotations" whose purpose is inspiration and encouragement.

• Redefinition of problems and breaking down their solutions into a step-by-step process.

• Modeling by the counselor in presence, style, behavior, or style of communication of attributes or values.

• Inspiration of new images, metaphors, ideals, affirmations, visualizations, stories, symbols, conceptualizations through which—through which—the counselee's internal conversation, the ongoing conversation that he holds with himself or herself, which she identifies as "me," "what I think, believe, feel," "who I am," my "self," in other words, the internal conversation in which she locates and experiences her identity as the self-conscious source and agent of feelings, thoughts,

actions, values, and meaning—through which the
counselee's internal conversation or identity is enriched,
enlarged, enhanced, ennobled.

I'm defining identity here phenomenologically rather
than metaphysically. My image of consciousness comes
from William James—the notion of consciousness as a
"stream" of images, ideas, voices, feeling tones, attitudes, reveries, all with multiple penumbras. The "current" of the stream, that is, the selfsame process with an
internally recognizable consistency perduring through
time I call "identity." The best descriptions of the nature
of the "stream of consciousness" are found in stream
of consciousness novelists such as Joyce in *Ulysses* or
Faulkner in *The Sound and the Fury*. I think the most
phenomenologically accurate way to describe this "identity" is as an internal talk or conversation shifting back
and forth between monologue and dialogue. Like the
current of a river this conversation is sometimes strong
and directive, as when we struggle with identity issues,
as defined by the DSM—long-term goals, career choice,
friendship patterns, sexual orientation and behavior,
religious identification, moral value systems, and group
loyalties—while at other times this "current" is almost
"unconscious" or imperceptible as it merges with the
more encompassing stream of consciousness.

It is this "identity" that we acknowledge when we
complain about noise so loud that "we can't hear ourselves think." Additionally, phenomenologically, there
are those moments when under duress, while in crisis,
or feeling shock or surprise, we consciously "talk to
ourselves" with verbal instructions such as "Stay calm,"

or "Don't panic," or "Focus," or "Think," or "What am I feeling now?" or "What's going on here?" or "Watch his right, watch his right," and thus seem to "externalize" our identity in order to give it intensity, thrust, or form as if we were dipping an oar into the current to push off from it, adding extra momentum. The Self or identity to which this talking is addressed is not another Self who overhears it, but the Self who we're about to become, merging back into the stream of consciousness the way an actor might merge back into the play—the ongoing monologue or dialogue, after having delivered a soliloquy for which, in terms of the action of the play itself, there is no audience. We externalize our "identities" or "selves" in varying degrees in almost every conversation, but most completely in those intimate conversations in which "we bare our souls," with our identities becoming "present" and thus vulnerable. These externalizations occur almost any time we are speaking or we believe that what is being said applies or is addressed to us. This is why words can hurt, wound, damage, or traumatize, but also soothe, calm, help, restore, uplift, transport, support, and heal.

The interventions listed above originate in a multitude of schools—client-centered therapy, behavior therapy, Gestalt, cognitive-behavioral therapy, REBT therapy, cognitive therapy, social work, reality therapy, structural and strategic approaches, MRI and deShazer-style interventions, psychodynamics, Adlerian and Franklian and existential therapies, developmental psychology, Ericksonian and hypnotic therapies. A good counselor, it seems to me, ought to at least try, within the ordinary human limits of time and ability, to maintain a friendly and more or less, with allowance for human limitations, up-to-date familiarity with all of them, supplemented by intense study and training when accessible.

To be a good counselor, then, you strive for an almost encyclopedic knowledge (life experience, plus training, plus knowledge of the theories and techniques of counseling from every school) expressed through a conversation, a style of language powerful and comprehensive enough in its appeal to the whole person that it invites the kind of emotional identification that fosters assimilation.

Now in thinking about this and looking for a "truth" to emerge from within my own experience, it seems to me that the best example I can come up with is the example of listening to Van Morrison, whom I like to listen to, emotionally identify with his music, and know nearly all of his lyrics by heart.

I would submit that the closest analogue to the learning process and uplifting transformation that occurs in psychotherapy may be the process that many of us undergo, each afternoon, sitting in rush-hour traffic or breezing along the highway home, singing along with the music on the radio, learning it, almost despite ourselves, absorbing the beat and rhythm into levels of the biochemistry of our brain, the psychophysical unity of our organism, entering into a kind of trancelike state, where we are happier, freer, more emotional, more in touch with our emotions, often recovering a memory either consciously or subconsciously; that is, it is present. So counselor as rock star—maybe? But there has to be a little more, doesn't there? There is, I think, although

I might be presumptuous thinking so, and given the choice between getting rid of rock music or psychotherapy, I know what most folks would choose, including my children.

The more, the extra, the *lagniappe*, as they say in New Orleans, is knowledge.

And what is a rock star plus knowledge plus a genuinely healing inspirational message?

Why, he or she is a bard, a romantic poet . . . like Wordsworth says, "A youthful Druid taught in shady grove / Primeval mysteries, a Bard elect."

In short, and ridiculously, I know—we're getting wildly grandiose here, but the phenomenological idea has always been that "extremes reveal essences"; that is, by going to extremes we're most likely to discover truly human truths. In short, if you want to practice effectively, like Yeats says, "take Homer as your theme." Strive to be an epic poet.

Homer, the poet—the epic poet.

In a traditional society epic poetry was not read. It was a magical, rhythmical, poetic, wide-ranging, instructive experience that was undergone, emotionally identified with, and then, as we would say, "internalized," so that Homer was not a "poet" in our sense, that is, the self-conscious creator of an autonomous, aesthetically perfect art object, isolated from a continuum of discourse; instead Homer was a state of mind that became, through the transmission and recitation of the epic, the state of mind of Greece, of nearly everyone in Greece.

Homer, to Greece, was a little like the Beatles and Bob Dylan, rolled up into one, were to the 60s—a state of mind.

But more, but more.

In what follows I draw almost exclusively on the work of the great classical scholar Eric Havelock in his *Preface to Plato*.

Who was the bard?

First and foremost he was an educator, whose work was fundamentally didactic. His job was to:

> . . . supply metrical encyclopedias. The poet is a source on the one hand of essential information, and the other essential moral training. Historically speaking, his claims even extend to giving technical instruction . . .

An educator, who also healed:

> . . . the regularity of the performance had a certain effect of hypnosis which relaxed the body's tensions and so also relaxed mental tensions, the fears, anxieties, and uncertainties which are the normal lot of our moral existence. Fatigue was temporarily forgotten and perhaps the erotic impulses, no longer blocked by anxiety, were stimulated.

Through a psychophysical unified process of total emotional identification:

> . . . its character can be summed up if we describe it as a state of total personal involvement and therefore of emotional identification with the substance of the poeticized statement that you are required to retain.

With the "event" of the process:

> In short, the artist identified with his story and the audience identified with the artist.

In which the bard was completely involved:

> He sank his personality in his performance. His audience in turn would remember only as they entered effectively and sympathetically into what he was saying . . .

That was completely internalized by the listener:

> . . . You threw yourself into the situation of Achilles, you identified with his grief or his anger . . . You yourself became Achilles and so did the reciter to whom you listened. Thirty years later you could automatically quote what Achilles had said or what the poet had said about him.

Psychologically, it is an act of personal commitment, of total engagement and of emotional identification to create in him a new state and frame of mind.

You did not learn your ethics and politics, skills and directives, by having them presented to you as a corpus for silent study, reflection and absorption. You were not asked to grasp their principles through rational analysis. You were not invited to as much as think of them. Instead you submitted to the . . . spell. You allowed yourself to become "musical" . . .

What allowing yourself to become "musical" meant was that as an audience member you experienced the "poetry" in such a way that you completely emotionally identified with it and internalized its meanings, content, symbols, their interrelations and style. You became it, it became you, you left forever altered.

Let me repeat this all again, sans quotations, and ask you to ask yourself if this doesn't sound a lot like psychotherapy, especially, and ironically, when psychotherapy is vilified by its enemies who, more than ourselves, understand the didactic function of psychotherapy exercised through the enchantment of music, the total identification on the part of its patients with its rhetorical and persuasive appeal.

The bard is an educator, who heals, through a process of, an act of personal commitment and emotional identification, with the event of the process, itself pleasurable, in which the bard is completely involved—that is, internalized—to create a new, and we might add, more integrated and better socialized, or as the Greek said, "musical" frame of mind.

Rock musician *cum* bard. That's my image of a counselor, what we have to strive for. As Yeats said, "Homer is my example, and his unchristened heart / The lion and the honeycomb, what has Scripture said?"

Another analogue, in addition to the example of the epic poetry performance, but closer to home, to the learning process that occurs in counseling, is the transformation that once occurred in churches all across Christendom, and continues to inspire and uplift congregations in African-American and white Pentecostal services every Sunday. As the performance of the epic poem transformed the Greeks, so in the Christian Church the sermon is the vehicle for shaking and reordering the soul's foundations.

Parallels exist between the Greek epic and the Christian sermon. Both poet and preacher, in a state of "trance" or emotional excitement, improvise, like a jazz or blues musician, upon inherited materials which for the poet are the myths, and for the preacher are the poetry and teachings of the Bible, as well as the "performances" of their forebears, colleagues, and rivals, to create an exultation of sound and sense in whose rhythmical elaboration the "audience" or congregation totally and integrally participate, immersed physically and intimately, responsorially, mouthing the familiar words along with the poet, or exclaiming with and to the preacher, to create and undergo, poet and auditor, preacher and congregation alike, a memorable, meaningful experience, with which they identify and which they internalize to become a new kind of man or woman—better, wiser, more integrated, both intra-psychically and into history and community.

But my focus here, and reason for adding the preacher to the rock musician and the epic poet in an attempt to clarify the changes that occur in counseling, is the effect of the sermon on its audience, which I propose to examine through the example of Dr. Martin Luther King.

Dr. King grew up a preacher's kid, spellbound by pulpit oratory. The sermons that he heard, with their rolling and rhapsodic rhythms, their powerful Biblical imagery, their moral imperatives and claims, enthralled him. Many of these sermons were almost songs; in their most exalted flights they approached the condition of a lyric. Garry Wills explains:

> The sermon verges always on music, picking up on the singing that preceded it and looking forward to the hymn that will follow. In a volume of the recorded *Riverside History of Classic Jazz*, a 1926 sermon illustrates this beautifully. The Rev. J.M. Gates of New York recites the words of a spiritual, announcing that the congregation is going to sing the song. Then, while he explicates and paraphrases the hymn, parishioners hum snatches of it, unable to wait, the tension mounting. At last he sings out the first verse, joined by the congregation. Then he plays verbal variations on the thought, in phrases of similar length and intonation, building up to the second verse . . .

> The interpenetration of song and sermon goes back to fourth-century Milan, to St. Ambrose. We find it in the sermons of St. Augustine, delivered before his volatile North African audiences. It is not surprising that A.D. Williams, Mike King, and Martin Jr. were all singers before they

became preachers . . . Their sermons had very
strong musical features—refrains, like those in
the blues; syncopated variations on the refrain;
phrases punctuated by cries from the worshipers;
quiet overtures; crescendos and accelerandos,
recapitulating codas.

Dr. King made of these sermons a lifelong study. Wills
describes him in the seminary:

The sermon, like jazz, is capable of the utmost
sophistication in what it can incorporate . . .
the readings that left their traces on King's
later writing were *sermons* that he read in the
seminary. Some authors of these sermons were
well known (like Harry Emerson Fosdick) but
others are quite obscure today (like J. Wal-
lace Hamilton or Thomas Butterick). The more
abstract theologians affected King's thought
only to the extent that those men's ideas had
been absorbed by the white *preachers* King read
and imitated. Only in sermon form did religious
thought inspire King. He did his school exercises, as a jazz musician might perform his scales
at a classical musical conservatory; but he came
alive only when the classical devices were put in
a jazz idiom.

And, then, at the end of his life, at the foot of the Lin-
coln Memorial, with his footsteps already beginning to
echo down the corridors of history, he rose to the top
of his profession, a preacher catapulted by his courage
and convictions to the heights of frame, the bright and
gleaming mountaintop where he espied a lost America
redeemed and recovered in love, through the sublime

and glorious vantage point of timeless truths intoned in his ageless oratory.

Now these sermons that Dr. King heard as a boy, studied in seminary and gave throughout his life became his consciousness; they "composed"—the word is apt—his identity. The sermons that he heard became his sermons; their rhythms, his rhythms; their images; his images; their forms and gestures, the forms and gestures into which he shaped himself. These sermons got into his blood, so that over time, he became of one mind with them, until their motifs and cadences became his mind— Dr. King became himself to the extent that they began to exercise a moral claim upon him. Wills writes:

> Martin King, like Cicero's ideal orator, marshaled all his resources—his learning, vocal exercises, physical bearing, memorization—to the effective address of his chosen audience. He tried to lift others up, and found himself lifted up in the process. He literally talked himself into useful kinds of trouble.

So soaked, steeped, and saturated in this experience and idiom of the sermon, so completely at one with it, Dr. King, in a sense became it, became its embodiment, a living testament and expression of it, so that when confronting any human situation or dilemma, it was not the wisdom of this tradition that "came" to him, as if his identity existed somehow separate from it; rather he was that wisdom, he was wise in it, thinking as it thought, believing as it believed and acting accordingly. In an exceptionally brilliant and compelling analysis of Dr. King's "I Have a Dream" speech, Wills shows that notwithstanding the fact that Dr. King could be, with reason, said to have "stolen" almost every trope and rhythm in it, yet it was totally, completely, inimitably his. He made it so. The creation of his consciousness, his ego, his lifelong immersion in the sensuous, transformative element of other preachers' words did not abolish or negate his individuality, but rather revealed it to be what it already was, what it ultimately is for every human being—a pulse of being, a basic attitude to life, a primordial "yes" or "no" to God's love and commandments to us.

Academics officiously sniff at Dr. King's imputed plagiarism. But the very idea of plagiarism, the act of which one solitary isolated self "steals," that is uses without attribution, the autonomous self-contained verbal units of another solitary isolated self—the very idea of plagiarism betrays a prejudice of print over oral culture, of men and women who locate their identities and meaning in books as opposed to what they do or say. The stigma attached to plagiarism serves as well the interests of a commercial society that is eager to reduce every value to the status of a commodity over which an owner may retain and exercise property rights.

Dr. King was not a plagiarist. Rather, he simply was his sources; he had become them and was no more capable of distinguishing between himself and them, his originality and theirs, than a ray of light feels the need to distinguish between itself and the sun—it is simply the sun's manifestation in space and time, an individual revelation of its beauty and life-giving power. If you're not a Church-goer, it's hard to fathom this. Its hard to

fathom the meaning of the education received by Dr.
King, of how it transforms you at the very heart of your
identity and being, so that you become "its" expression,
"its" creation, "its" voice without losing your own individuality, but instead having your individuality crowned
and enhanced. If you've never sat with the congregation, crowded into hard, wooden, stiff-backed pews, the
children noisy and squirming, the windows propped
open onto an endless blue sky and the lush greenness
of June meadows, the fresh scent of new-mown hay
drifting over, the fan above whirring, clickety-clackety,
clickety-clackety, the hymnals on the laps already open
to the next song, the ladies all in their Sunday finest,
with hand fans and handkerchiefs to dab inconspicu-
ously at tiny beads of sweat, and then a hush falls over
the sanctuary, like heaven's own sweet breath, the still-
ness before creation, as the preacher dressed in flowing
robes solemnly walks to the lectern—if you've never sat
at a service like this, it's hard to credit or understand the
meaning of Dr. King's life and career.

But imagine it, if you will, the preacher reaching the
podium now—

Starting slow, he falters, mumbles, can't find his place.
Mops his brow. Steps back from the podium. Invites his
brethren to identify with him, his humility, mortality, his
vulnerable human presence.

The preacher walks and talks across the stage. Presses
hard—too hard. Strains. He just can't get it, but then a
rhythm catches him. He airs it out. The congregation
starts a singsong croon, to sweetly mumble in answer to

him. The older people do it first, especially the women, regal in their creased and crow's feet dignity.

The preacher starts his climb; the rhythms mount. He hikes up the mountaintop of every human heart, shimmies up the rain gutter to the very rooftop of the world. The stars come out in every sentence. He's Jeremiah thundering denunciations. He's Samson with the jawbone of an ass. He's David strumming gently his spiritual harp, bringing joy, bringing joy, bringing joy—quieting the madness, shepherding the sheep.

And then he's there, he's there—one with the Lord. The Glory of the Lord shines all around him. His golden phrases flash like a meteor shower. He's a fire on the mountain; a choir in the air; a horse stampede on a crowded street; a hound that's treed his prey. He's a flood in the Delta; a hurricane on the coast; he's the stone that rolls away—and the congregation's right there with him. The air's electric hair stands on end. The children can't believe it; they stop their fidgeting.

Sunday polished shoes or work boots shuffle on hardwood floors. Shoulders shake and shiver. Everyone's singing and shouting and joining in. For twenty minutes, more or less, they all walk hand in hand in glory.

Then he starts his slow descent, inching down the mountainside foothold by foothold, down the steep face of a cliff, until they're back to where they started. They sink back into the pew in silent meditation, some forever changed by the power of the sermon, the change taking hold in their heart. Some, though lifted by the language, fall back swiftly into their old routines and ways.

"May the words of the mouth and the meditations of my heart . . . " The last syllable fades. They pass through the Church doors out into the light, "Good sermon, Preacher."

A Christian baptized weekly, as it were, or more likely, three or four times weekly in these festivals of God's Word is no more capable of distinguishing between his "ego," "self," or "identity," and the sermons he has heard, his originality and theirs, than was Dr. King.

It's very difficult, as I said, for a nonbeliever or a non-Church-goer, or a non-goer to this kind of Church, to understand the changes in the heart and soul and consciousness of a Christian that these kinds of sermons can effect. It's equally hard for we moderns to project ourselves back in time with sufficient intensity to grasp the full meaning and sense of the epic poet's performance. But it is also difficult—is it not?—for people who have never experienced the impact of a long-term psychotherapy to credit the transformations that can occur with it. About counseling's effects, many continue to be mystified and skeptical, at best, or outright dismissive at worst.

I would argue that a close similarity binds poet, preacher, and counselor. They are of oratory all compact. The form of counseling may be more "conversational" in structure than the epic poem or sermon, although, as I have tried to show, both of these forms are more involving and co-creative than is often thought, but the function in counseling is as directive and determining as any poem or sermon. I would accept a comparison between counseling and Socratic dialogue, but the idea that Socratic dialogues are in any respect anything resembling "collaborative conversations" is soon debunked by performing them live and out loud. Most of Socrates' interlocutors actually say very little, while Socrates talks a lot, coaxing and goading his protégés along in an intended line of inquiry, tempering his rather aggressive questioning with beautiful turns of phrase, myths, stories, and frequent lofty, lyrical interludes of speech.

Talk. Talk. I like the word "talk" as in the "talking cure" much better than "conversation" as a description of psychotherapy. A talk can be a one-man show or a two-way street. "A good talking to" down South, implies moral upbraiding and instruction. "Talking it through" means getting somewhere, to a new place of insight and understanding, or a feeling of comfort. "Talking it over" is a collaborative exploration. "All talked out" suggests there are limits to speech, while subtly underlining the fact that speech is a behavior that draws on all our psychophysical resources to drain them and tire us out. "Talk to me" means to emotionally connect, validate, confirm. "Talk about it" evokes the need for expression of feeling and feeling identification. "Talk it out" implies conflict resolution. Big talk. All talk. Talk to me. Walk with me. I can't stand the way he sings, but I love the way he talks, as they say up on Cripple Creek, with the Band, about Spike Jones.

Does this scare you—the idea that a counselor must be a poet? Or a preacher? Perhaps the image of the coun-

selor as poet, healing through the music and rhythm
of his talk, a member of the fraternity and visionary
company of bards, scares you??? And the image of the
preacher—if you're not already involved in pastoral
counseling, perhaps the notion of a family resemblance
existing between counselor and preacher seems even
more far-fetched.

I'll leave behind, then, these presumptuous notions, but
ones that nonetheless, if taken with a grain of salt, and
big heaping dose of self-mockery, has great relevance to
the formation of the counselor's identity and the essence
of the healing process.

So good-bye to all that, to rock stars and *The Iliad* and
fried green tomatoes, southern tub-thumping preacher-
style oratory, to say only—

That what occurs in therapy is a special kind
of conversation.

In a special state of mind or mood.

That I would call "truthful" in the existentialist sense.

That I would call "poetry" or "music" in the Greek
sense, the music and poetry of counseling, the heart
and soul of counseling, full of both meaning and spirit,
or, if you must, the "process" or "narrative" or "story"
of counseling.

Which the counselee, gradually, over time, internalizes,
so that where before existed an internal conversation or

identity, that may have been ashamed, punitive, constricted, despairing, overwhelmed, compulsive, emotionless, impoverished or distorted in affect or cognition, etc., there now exists, as a result of the counseling process, emotional identification, as it were, with its music and poetry, a new conversation or identity more tolerant, relaxed, graceful, understanding, expressive, resourceful, creative, informed, flexible, erotic, assertive, etc.

The process that through several metaphors I am describing, by which a client changes through internalization of the process of "talk" therapy occurs only in varying degrees. The risk of "brainwashing" is nonexistent. Unlike the poet who speaks for the divine, or the preacher who speaks for God and is invested with Her authority, the therapist is just a person who despite her "authority" remains just a person whose simple humanity and feet of clay, mistakes and misunderstandings, are inevitably revealed through the course of the counseling. It is this human relationship binding client and therapist that creates the possibility of change, while also limiting it. If the counselor is comfortable with his own humanity and if the counseling relationship is given adequate time to mature into genuineness and friendship, what the counselor "says" becomes just that, "what my counselor says"—often on target, worth thinking about, but not infallible. The "poetic" and "preacherly" dimensions of the relationship become something identified and integrated into the relationship, as in "my imagination is really running wild here, but . . . " or "I know I'm preaching to you now, but I've got something I need to preach about." To the client the counselor becomes someone who can sound like a poet

or preacher at times, but someone who remains just a
guy, doing the best he can, sitting across the room, with
whom one is involved in a very intense, informative,
and, perhaps, inspiring conversation.

What changes as a result of counseling, then? A counselee's identity defined as an ongoing internal conversation. How does it change? It is enriched and enlarged.
I would also add "truthful" and here separate myself
from my "constructivist" colleagues, and "rational with
understanding." More existentialist, more spiritual, more
capable of generating "truth" through trust in phenomenological attunement to its own process. How does this
happen? Through internalization of the special conversation that occurs in counseling. The music of counseling, its heart and soul, is learned by and taken to heart
producing a change of heart that may or may not endure.

The Irish call this kind of conversation "the crack":

> In Ireland, the Divine is nourished by conversa-
> tion. At its best, Irish talk retains a sacramental
> quality and so needs no other justification. Like
> any creative act, or rather *the* Creation of the
> gods, "the crack" is understood as a primary
> event. In its stream, idea, emotion, and thing
> combine in whirlpools (whose equivalent in tra-
> ditional Irish music are jigs and reels) alternating
> with placid stretches and furious falls. At times
> submerged cargoes, long supposed lost, rear up,
> waterlogged yet intact, to bump and nuzzle in the
> ceaseless flow. Such supernatural talk is no mere
> description or illustration of a parallel reality. It *is*
> the Other, returned to life—a life made between

> speaker and listener (who exchange roles, turn
> by turn) and where eye and gesture contribute
> like the glitter of sunlight on a wind-stirred loch,
> to the business of serious delight." (Michael
> Dames, *Mythic Ireland*, p. 72.)

Glib, smooth, silver-tongued, barfly, bartender, barber,
beautician, Socrates, epic poet, philosophy, bull and bull
shit, shoot the breeze, good blarney, talk about it, talk it
over, talk it through, talk it out, say it ain't so, say it is,
gossip, jokes, stories, direction, advice, connections, insight, guidance, who knows who, good information and
valid points, poetry, music, confession, dialogue, vent-
ing, healing, crack, talk your ear off, talk a blue streak,
talked to death, talked to life, all talked out, tears spill,
heart flows, river rises—crack—good conversation, good
session, counseling.

I ask you if thinking that you might have to be a poet or
a preacher scares you?

But perhaps this scares you more. Perhaps it's more
intimidating to suggest that therapeutic effectiveness
may depend most on the counselor's artfulness in conversation, the abundance and energy of his ideas and
insights, his sensitivity and intelligence, than it is to
assert that the counselor must be a poet, since that ideal
seems so grandiose, so effetely literary, and so incom-
patible with the experience most of us have with our
colleagues who always seem so good at active listening.
But artful talk??—having to talk for an hour, hour after
hour, having enough to say, enough that's interesting
or valuable or entertaining or worth anybody's time and
money—now, that's scary.

Jay Haley has some wonderful things to say about therapy and talk. He has some great fun with the fact that the primal fear of nearly all therapists, whether novice or experienced, is not that we will not know what to do about a problem or symptom, or that our advice, directives, or interpretations will prove ineffectual or in error or even damaging to the client; no, the primal fear, for all of us, is that we will run out of things to say or ask and won't be able to fill the hour. As time ticks by we'll just have to sit there looking dumb, as our case-loads shrink and our practices become more private than we would care for them to be. Haley writes:

> It is in relation to teaching clients about themselves that I discovered the most important question about therapy that is asked by beginning trainees. They may be exposed to psychodynamics, or behavior therapy, or family therapy, or directive therapy, but one question they ask is at the heart of these choices and determines their questions. What is that question? . . . The question every trainee must ask is, "When I see a client or a family, what can I talk about for a whole hour? What do I say to them?"
>
> Different schools of therapy stand or fall on how this question is answered.

I am saying that counselors heal through the productivity and energy and delight of their talk.

I would further say that in response to any given situation, the choice that a counselor makes from available interventions, which, from my eclectic, integrative, multi-modal point of view, includes the techniques and theories of all the schools, stacked up like a sheaf of musical scores to be selected according to the needs and the mood of the moment, must be made according to what will open up the richest vein of conversation. If subsequent to any intervention, the conversation "dies," which does not automatically equate with silence—silence can be pensive, thought-ful, anticipatory, pregnant, or expressive—if it fails to pick up steam, or open onto new vistas or topics, then the intervention probably failed. This is really not so far from the old psychoanalytic idea that the best interpretation is not necessarily the one that most ac-curately identifies unconscious conflicts or emotions, but the one that releases further unconscious mate-rial, with the difference that my view, it seems to me, sticks more to the phenomena and is less buried under superfluous theory.

I've proposed a theory of change, of how change occurs in counseling and of what actually is changed. Let me also give you a brief, thumbnail sketch of my "theory" of personality and theory of neurosis; that is, my ex-planation, or working hypothesis of why it is we suffer. And then, as I warned you earlier, a political statement.

Personality—is it dreams, sugar and spice, or puppy dogs' tails that we're made of? For maintaining my bal-ance in counseling, I use this rule of thumb—

Going down, from outside in, from least important to most, like steps down into a catacomb:

On the first step, well, we're just what others make us, or socialize us into: we're learned behaviors, internalized scripts, social codes, taboos, expectations, which are sometimes autonomously enduring but are more typically sustained and reinforced by repetitive communication and behavioral interactional sequences that escape attention and awareness. We're clichés governed by the laws of association and homeostasis.

Van Morrison has a song called "Thanks for the Information" whose verses are cliché after cliché that purport to explain life or govern appropriate action in human situations. The refrain is about, given all this drivel, how it's marvelous and magical that we can even make it through.

On the second step, or level, or dimension, are feelings, emotions, affects, and also memory and imagination, the *sensus communis* in traditional language.

Third is what we are by nature and species and organism, stimulus and response, and evolution. Here we are passion, appetite, instinct. This is the part of us that eats, drinks, voids, sleeps, mates, reproduces, preserves itself through the fight-or-flight mechanism. It is amoral, absent scruples.

Fourth, at or in the zone, is the abyss of ourselves. We are persons, spirits, self-conscious free entities, endowed with inalienable rights and normative responsibilities whose existence is always a coexistence, that is, in relationship to the "Other."

Now to dynamically describe the characteristic dynamisms or energy that exist within this "field" of personality.

The first level is *fixed*; it restrains, checks, holds back, limits, arrests, inhibits, repeats, and maintains.

The second level of feelings, memories, and imagination *flow*—they dissolve, engulf, release, renew, deepen, but feelings can also form in the sense that they provide the energy and determination for setting limits, creating and asserting boundaries.

The third level *surges*, seeking satisfaction and completion, usually defined as absent displeasure or tension. It tumesces, swells, flexes, thrusts, tipples and stipples, moistens, presses for relief.

And, finally, the fourth level is as *fixed* as a question whose clarity and unwavering tension puts a claim on us that we experience to be absolute and as freeing as the completion and resumption of uninterrupted *flow* that comes with an answer truly given.

The question, of course, addressed to us at the deepest level, is the question addressed to our freedom of whether or not to affirm our karma, our calling, our fate or destiny, what it is that life wants from us or asks from us, which for the Christian is the calling to fulfill oneself through the two great commandments of loving others as ourselves and loving God with body, mind, and soul.

We love others best by realizing that the one who sees, that is, a self-conscious being with an irreplaceable ontological value, is also seen by other beings with an equal value, an equal depth, meaning and mystery, who is unlike "me" in not being me but equal to me in onto- logical value and thus related to me in being like me in ultimate importance. This is the revelation and the radi- ance of the "Other" as an expressive human face.

À la Yeats' example in *A Vision,* I sometimes try to fix these levels more decisively in memory by describing them through symbols.

The first level—the level of ordinary consciousness and behavior, the level of *Das Mann* in Heideggerian lan- guage—is the *Mask*. For Jungians, it is the Persona.

The second level of feelings, memory, and imagination is the *Heart*, to whose "uplifting" I devote most of my clinical efforts. This is the Jungian Anima and Animus.

The third level of instincts and drives is the *Daimon*, the Jungian Shadow and Underworld (see Rollo May's *Love and Will* for a splendid discussion of the daimonic and its relationship to the healing Word).

Just here, I might interject, in the intercourse between the *Heart* and the *Daimon* occurs the great romantic temptation to argue that the "imagination" is itself an instinct, a primal urge in life, daimonic in nature, in terms of which, as is the case with sexuality and ag- gression, everything else can be understood or usefully insighted. I would argue that this is true only for genuine artists who do feel a "compulsion" to create and are genuinely daimonic, driven women or men. Memory and dream and imagination are more typically less daimonic and driven, less compulsive, and in the experiential claim that they make upon us, more analogous to feelings. The romantic temptation is to believe, on the basis of our own occasional "creativity" that we are all somehow "artists" or that the "psyche" is, and to construct a psychology upon this principle. To read or hear ourselves described as potential "artists" is flattering, but for the vast majority of us, inaccurate. The best guide on this distinction is Alfred Adler, who while recognizing the "fictional" aspect of consciousness, insisted always on the "uniqueness" of the artist, while simultaneously emphasizing the "iron logic" and reality of human life.

The fourth, the deepest and most significant, is the *Person*, the Jungian Self, Viktor Frankl's "noosphere," that deep cistern within all of us that Bernanos talks about, who self-actualizes through relationships with that which transcends it.

All of the major psychological models and theories can be appreciated, and to some degree, synthesized, in terms of this approach. Cognitive-Behaviorists, REBT, systems, transactional and interactional, and collaborative theories give the best accounts of how the irrational assumptions and automatic thoughts of ordinary consciousness and the dysfunctional sequences and patterns of typical behavior impair adaptation and functioning while deterring psychological growth.

Rogers and Satir illuminate the second level of feelings. To memory and imagination, Hillman is the best guide. The French phenomenological philosopher Gaston Bachelard is also helpful, as are the "Directed Daydream" psychotherapies of Robert Desoille and Hanscarl Leuner. But of very greater value, it seems to me, for grasping the place of memory and imagination in human life and judgment are various amplifications of the Thomistic and traditional idea of the "phantasm." The best of these is Frederick D. Wilhelmsen's essay "The Philosopher and the Myth" found in his *The Paradoxical Structure of Existence*, and later, in less detail, in his coauthored book with Janet Bret, *Telepolitics*.

Freud, Jung, Adler, and Nietzsche, sociobiology, evolutionary psychology, also Perls, and May to some extent, speak for the *Daimonic*.

The existential, humanistic, transpersonal and spiritual psychologies are most helpful in understanding the *Person*.

The only psychological theorists with whom I am familiar who attempted a genuine synthetic account of all the levels were William James and Henry Murray, primarily I think, because their work antedated, or in the case of Murray independently paralleled, the division of psychology into "schools," whose effect upon their partisans is inevitably to limit the ability to synthesize their original perspective into a larger, more integrative framework.

The tension and conflicts that exist in this personality field generate *character*. Our character develops through the action of affirmation, and further actions that express these affirmations of our relationship to God and the transcendence of the Other, of our natures and of nature itself, including its voids of non-being such as pain, cruelty, illness and death, which are affirmed as a meaningful and even beautiful part of the struggle, even as we struggle against them. Affirmation of the reality of our feelings and the crucial value and comforting, transformative value of our memories, dreams, and imagination, and affirmations of our traditions, culture, history, and society insofar as they are consistent with our affirmations of God, Nature, our interior life of feelings, and insofar as they are not, character develops through opposition and resistance.

This would be a romantic-Christian and spiritual existential definition of character, one to which even Lord Byron and St. Augustine might give their assent.

I hope it's clear by now that my approach belongs to the humanistic therapies in that its main efforts are directed at removing the fixities or blockages of the first level for the sake of the self-actualization that occurs when the soul begins to flow and form with feelings, and to surge with passion and the glow of organic cohesion and health.

I pitch my tent most visibly in the humanistic camp on the question of "feelings." I follow von Balthasar (*The Glory of the Lord*, Volume V, p. 298) in his defense of the modern notion of "feeling" which he traces in the Scot philosophers, Shaftesbury, Goethe, and Rosseau, as an extension of the doctrine of the "spiritual senses" developed by the Fathers and Doctors of the Church in order to emphasize the essential goodness of ordinary embodied life upon the earth. Obviously, von Balthasar considers the romantic emphasis on feelings wholly legitimate. It seems to me that almost alone among contemporary therapies it is Humanistic Psychology that consistently emphasizes the critical importance of feelings and of "emotional intelligence" in human life and thus remains in continuity with the older tradition.

James Hillman is particularly hard on what he calls "the romantic cult of feelings" which, with only modest historical justification, he traces back to St. Augustine's *Confessions*. In a fit of anti-Christianism and over-intellectualized Platonic snobbery, Hillman pits imagination against the subtleties of affective life:

> Let us notice at once that this intimate heart of feelings is not the heart of the Greeks, or of the Hebrews, or of the Persian thought . . . And this heart of subjective feeling holds imagination in its captivity. We judge our images in terms of their feelings. Whether a project or reverie be imagined further is determined by how it feels. Is this dream good or bad—feeling will tell you . . .

By pitting imagination against feelings Hillman departs from the main Romantic tradition of which he is so often such an able and eloquent exponent. In the Romantic tradition, feelings and imagination are indissolubly, inseparably joined, as heart and soul, as pulse and breath.

The cult of feeling is at the core of my counseling. I routinely ask children and teenagers to keep "feeling books," coloring them or emblazoning them with colors, sequins, stickers, photographs, and images that are important to them, or that they just find aesthetically appealing, in which each day they try to keep track and record some of their feelings, as in pages with the headings "I felt sad this week . . . " "When . . . " "It made me think of . . . " "I noticed that into my mind came . . . " or "I wanted to . . . " With adults I do more or less the same, asking them to keep a feeling journal. I structure most of my sessions with feeling queries about "Can you tell me about a time this week when you felt angry, sad, anxious, lonely, unattached, etc?" and in a pinch these are always the questions I come back to. In relationship counseling the discrimination of feeling through "I feel" statements plays a major role.

I am a member of the "romantic cult of feelings." For me feelings are "the spiritual senses." I believe inside of us, below the surface that may seem calm or rigid, there exists an extraordinary wealth of feelings, a treasure of emotions, a differentiated and complex attunement to the world. I like to image this world, teeming with marvels and exotica, creatures and discomforts, in fluid, quiet, dreamlike state.

Feelings—I'd like to be the Shakespeare or Augustine of feelings—and try to be so as much as I can in every session.

May I try that, for a moment, for you? Let me chant here—so it's the spirit rather than the letter of what I'm writing that must be present here—rhythm drunk, feeling drunk, naming as many kinds of feelings, emotions, and feeling-toned attitudes and subtle, emotion-filled perceptions of events, situations and states of mind as

I can. "I can call spirits from the vasty deep" said Owen Glendower, the great Welsh Captain and Wizard in Shakespeare's *Henry V*, to which Hotspur, the flower of English chivalry responds, "But do they come when you do call for them?"

They may not come. This exercise may seem silly. But it gives a taste of just how complex and differentiated our affective life truly is, or can be if we're inclined to name and know it, speak and stand for it. For me, as I just say and savor each of these words, my heart begins to dive and swim, and dive again all the way to the bottom . . .

Are you today, or have you this week felt—

Bored, trapped, under the gun, ready to get it over with?

Confused, on target, prickly, connected, frustrated, tired, forgetful, sleepy, can't sleep, blocked, menaced, hemmed in, distracted, weepy, humiliated, ancient, annoyed, concerned, out of place, unavailable, simple, grandiose, rotten, forgiving, respected, close to, intimate, rested, plastic, absorbed, can't breathe, ecstatic, can't move, controlled, like I wasn't there?

Glued to, intimidated, overcome, lost, head over heels, aghast, resentful, can't stop talking, starved, squeezed, on a pedestal, mistaken, walled off, wishy-washy, ganged up on, strong, in a trance, desperate, overwhelmed, pretty, nurtured, crucified, walked all over, scared, awkward, not there, silent, creepy, fluttery, wrong, right, speechless, withdrawn, stiff, cowardly, unpopular, wasted, snooty, fickle, comfortable, riled, indecisive, bowels in an uproar, miffed?

Dismayed, fingered, picked on, obsessed, desirable, invisible, stirred up, stoned, fearful, in dread, regretful, like an animal, dim, rageful, not sorry, depressed, encouraged, alone, completely alone, murderous, glacial, incompetent, disliked, tearful, guilty, free, helpless, incomplete, likeable, irritated, bloated, positive, in the woods, attacked, in the dark, caring, ashamed, fascinated, choked, on my last legs, out of it, explosive, coming apart, out of control, undone, beyond help, mechanical, reluctant, interested, all wet, furious, humble, in tune with, spilling over, wretched, pathetic, sunk, like a dog, impotent, pushed, pushed away, bitchy, followed, misunderstood, optimistic, pessimistic, throttled, squashed, frustrated, challenged, out on a limb, held back, happy, bothered, responsive, frigid, clever, manipulated, smitten, thrilled, fed up, pensive, safe, rueful, sterile, stalked, hesitant, aloof, hard, lame, brittle, unloved, swallowed whole, rabid, engulfed, moody, critical, judgmental, reserved, clingy, tormented, wacky, punished, clobbered, warm, crippled, demonstrative, huge, playful, terrific, soggy, experienced, left out, devastated, uncanny, made fun of, excited, uncomfortable, puzzled, watchful, inspired, astounded, unable to, replaced, intrusive, not serious, creative, relieved, dispossessed, effusive, militant, disturbed, impatient, storm-tossed, rigid, yellow, blue, cheerless, disgraced, calm, watched, controlled, unforgiving, dumb, like a fool, backed-up, disturbed, spent, hit on, harped on, lethargic, predictable, upset, goofy, loved, supported, unsupported, on hold, in between, grieving, stewing, down and dirty, friendly, burdened, in trouble, pitiful, mean, soiled, spoiled, abused, overextended, manipulative, guarded, victimized, used, used up, orgasmic, on the edge, frayed, drunk, miserable, attached, connected, simmering, sad, misunderstood, bitter, lonely, enmeshed, worse, distant, devious, criminal, divided, split, rent, heroic, dependable, invaded, decisive, caught in the middle, all mixed up, wired, fried, satisfied, pressured, sloppy, fresh, like a loser, excited, resurrected, listened to, on track, predictable, sensitive, damaged, determined, exploited, wonderful, committed, drained, put-off, surprised, taken advantage of, proud, demented, worthless, grim, stuffed, squelched, innocent, hopeful, silly, burnt, burnt out, neglected, ignored, downcast, sick, dumb, comforted, consoled, heartsick, broken hearted, unhappy, left behind, dejected, focused, wounded, bruised, traumatized, dreadful, suicidal, on a slow burn, nervous, jittery, numb, high, low, in the zone, injured, betrayed, receptive, like I'm starting over, guilty, hollow, like I'm dead, sexy, messy, jealous, joined at the hip, shocked, frantic, pursued, panicky, like shit, funked, shit on, exhausted, hurt, pissed, upbeat, beat up, in a rut, immature, chosen, clumsy, labeled, unexpected, harmed, abandoned, froze out, froze up, frightened, mean, damned, pushed, spineless, filled, appreciated, deficient, like throwing up, overestimated, cruel, dubious, malignant, dwarfed, remorseful, rejected, successful, doubtful, sorry, complete, tight, belittled, out of touch, out of step, jaded, unnerved, deceived, relieved, finished, at the end of my rope, blown away, squirming, seething, adventurous, teased, no choice, jerked around, jacked around, engrossed, feverish, at my breaking point, crummy, barely functioning, lovesick, overly sensitive, hanging

on, on the move, eaten up with, eaten alive, chewed up
and spit out, understanding, tied up, an attitude, bogged
down, reserved, gutty, catty, like crud, still stinging,
snippy, addicted, locked out, shut down, brain dead, out
of bounds, over-stimulated, failed, like a failure, weak,
fated, delicate, shot down, leaned on, seen through,
spiritual, knocked flat, dubious, punished, inferior,
superior, mesmerized, nailed, isolated, stimulated, concerned, like a fraud, competitive, tricked, fretful, stuck,
qualified, cut off, cut, dropped, overdrawn, worn down,
serious, oily, sleazy, fragile, give-out, tense, clueless,
like new, don't care, couldn't care less, roller coasting,
coasting, on the move, free ride, on the gravy train,
crabby, flying, seen through, like a hostage, appreciated,
okay, resigned, immune, stable, unstable, on my knees,
like talking, set up, avoided, pestered, whiny, manipulated, fetching, validated, selfish, stomped on, blown off,
withdrawn, embarrassed, self-centered, spooky, vain,
naked to the world, ragged, ragged out, exposed, ex-
cluded, daring, undeserving, testy, frisky, awful, defen-
sive, indefensible, on the defense, defenseless, involved,
conspiratorial, inside, in, cool, ugly, in the mood, vexed,
wronged, mellow, cheated, creamed, exasperated, don't
know where to turn, like a sponge, distressed, untouch-
able, like nobody cares, all alone, about to burst, flood-
ed, held back, ruined, on the run, burdened, complete,
imprisoned, daunted, a wreck, a fake, identified with,
lazy, passionate, forgotten, going strong, in the groove,
ridiculed, back from, feverish, thick, special, battered,
threatened, infatuated, cursed, can't stop . . .

Well, I'll stop—except to add mad, glad, sad, anxious
or depressed . . .

The development of feeling depends upon the sophistication of our feeling-language. It depends upon plenitude and subtlety. I'm not sure, despite the assumptions that most people make about our touchy-feely profession, that most counselors are actually, when it comes to feeling-language, very sophisticated at all. Once we get past mad, sad and glad, and add in maybe anxious, then the cat's got our tongue. As our feeling language grows richer, so too does our ability to help and heal.

As Hillman writes (proving in light of my last quotation from him the truth of Emerson's contention that "consistency is the hobgoblin of little minds")—

> Language of quality. I was very happy to hear that because I feel that the differentiation of language is part of making conscious these emotional turmoils, fears, panics, and so on. The philosopher Hegel said that there is not a single state of the soul or the mind that language cannot express. Poets do it all the time. I think the contemporary poverty of language in psychology makes feelings even more amorphous. I think that it is extremely important to consciousness that we can talk about qualities like "flutteriness," and elaborate them, staying close with them and not elaborating the feelings away, but staying with whatever quality is. Therapy should not forget the value in the human being of one's unique gift of language. We are the one species that has this kind of language, and that has the physiology, the anatomy for producing speech.

May I give you just a taste of how counseling as a "cult of feeling" translates into, and sounds, in an actual counseling exchange?

"Why do I hold on to this anger?" she asks tearfully.

It's been twelve years. She still feels the same as she did. She is married, with children (three), successful, educated, but very, very unhappy in her marriage. She wants a little bit of that "hot monogamy" that is so in vogue now, and which she thinks most of her friends are enjoying.

And, more than anything, she wants to get over her anger. She thinks anger is a fault; that she is still angry is her fault, a sign of some flaw or defect in her. Her religion, what she's been taught, or thinks she's been taught, everything she reads, all the common sense advice from her friends and family—everything, the "Script" says holding on to anger is bad and that you ought to let go of it.

I say: "You hold on to the anger first, because as St. Augustine said, anger is the first step to courage. And it's taken courage to do all that you've done, to take the little steps and the big steps, to risk the thought, and yes, thought is sometimes a risk, that you might end your marriage."

"You hold on to it too because you can't let go—nobody can of such deep hurt. When you say 'Why can't I just let the fact that I've had my feelings hurt so many times go?' it prejudges the question. Hurt feelings aren't really

that bad, you ought to be able to get over it, but it's not
just hurt feelings, it's much more. It's trauma. You know
if you've ever had a car accident, ten years or more can
pass, and if you're driving down the highway and the
conditions are just right, are very nearly the same as
they were ten years ago, if the car swerves just the same
or something triggers that reflex—you flinch, your heart
races, you catch your breath because though your mind
may have long since forgotten about the accident, or
you don't think of it very much, your body remembers.
That's the way it is with any trauma, something that
reaches down deep into your soul and burns and cuts
and wounds and shakes you up. It just stays with you,
you can't forget, can't just let go, because we're wired
that way. We have the self-preservation instinct in us,
the natural defense of our souls and worth—let that go
and there's nothing left. You can't forget because it's
your letter to yourself reminding you that you're worth
something, you're valuable, you're a child of God, you
count and God cares whether or not you're hurt. You
can't let go because, what will happen if you do let go?
Anger is the only emotion left perhaps, maybe nothing
else is, and then on the other side of anger, there's just
nothing. You know we talk a lot about our partners—it's
like living with a stranger, well it's not—when nothing else is left, at least they're familiar. You want to
know what's it's like to really live with a stranger? It's
nothing, absolutely nothing. It's riding the subway and
noticing that person next to you, that there's something
wrong with their appearance, something on, inside out
or something—and feeling not the slightest impulse or
inclination to say anything, just feel nothing, no connection, no caring, no nothing. Your anger at least keeps

him familiar, makes him something to you, and we all need someone to be something to us."

"Why do you think country music is so popular? It's about—or a lot of it is, how relationships can hurt and hurt real bad, not just when you're left behind or cheated on, but just about being high and lonesome, being lonely, wanting to miss somebody when they're not there, and wanting to be missed when you're not there."

"How can you forgive—you have to have him recognize your hurt, as he probably would if you weren't married, if you were on the TV, or someone at his office, or a story that he hears. You have to at least feel that he sees that you're hurt—not that he realizes that he caused it, that he did it to you, though that would be nice—and he need not ask forgiveness though that would be even better, you'll have to feel that somehow he sees it. I don't know if that will ever happen; it might, but it won't if you're not mad enough to keep working at it, keep connected, mad enough to scream and cry and shudder and give up and maybe break down and say the words—show you're hurt, show the loss."

I want her to hang on to that anger, feel it deeply, listen to it, treat it like a teacher and personal angel.

That's how this "humanistic" counseling sounds.

But my approach differs from the humanistic therapies, or more honestly, is frankly at odds with them, in its assumption that the definition or self-actualization for me is far less indeterminate than one finds with them;

instead, I believe that true actualization for human beings is found exclusively in imitation of the feminine
receptivity and innocence of the perfect submission of
Mary that allows Christ to come into our hearts, to be
born in our spiritual wombs and life-worlds.

My theory is that neurosis is implicit in these ideas
about the personality field. We suffer, mainly, because
the outer shell of personality, the rigidities and stupidities of our codes, scripts, clichés, and socializations
become so constrictive, overwhelming, and repressive
that we don't know who we are—don't know what and
who we are at the deepest and most intimate level of our
being, which occurs primarily through losing touch with
our desires and feelings, so that in any given human
situation to which we must make a response, we either
don't know what to do, that is, we are, in a literal sense,
ignorant; or knowing what to do, we are afraid to do it,
lacking even that desire and fire, balls and backbone,
guts and intestinal fortitude that ought to be instinctively given; or don't believe or understand that we remain
existentially free to choose that path despite whatever
obstacles might inhibit or deter us. This ignorance,
emptiness, hollowness, despair, discouragement, loss of
courage and passion, is then reinforced by rationalizations, which are themselves the internalized rules and
taboos of the social code.

Alienation from our natures occurs through socialization, first at the hands of parents, who out of fear or
rejection, or embarrassment, or ignorance, refuse to
tell their child "No," and instead, attempt to substitute
their own desires for the child's, as in living vicariously

through them, or more typically, through everyday communications such as "You don't want that, do you? Don't you want this?" or "I know why you're acting that way," or "You shouldn't want to do that." Later, this self-alienation is reinforced at school where good behavior is equated with conformity, and where passive compliance with the rules and authority is rewarded and praised.

The alternative to this is socialization, that is, a parenting and educational style that encourages a child to express and risk acting upon their own desires and feelings within the context of a human relationship, a rather flexible structure that allows them to tap into their own self-regulatory process. The price for this is a little inconvenience on the part of adults, but a healthy developmental process for children that progressively becomes a revelation of essence, of the "soul's code," as Hillman has described it, which, for the Christian, will be understood as our creation in the image of God, that is, the divine image in us whose potential is perfection through grace, while also remaining keyed to the claims and differentiations of human nature as experienced through our instinctual and affective lives.

Of course, discipline at times is necessary, but firm limits can be imposed within a relationship characterized by continuity and trust by a confident adult capable of saying "No." The fact is, however, that many of us as parents, and too much of our educational system "disciplines" by punitively pathologizing what are normal feelings and desires in children, while seductively en-

couraging through praise and reward, or threat of with-
drawal of affection, or abandonment, identification with
adult desires alien to the child's innate dispositions.

But even as I critique institutions and conventions, I
would also add, however, a very romantic awareness
of the duplicity and destruction, the daemonic aspect of
nature of that which are on the third level, biologically
and by nature. I do not equate neurosis with mental
illness. Mental illness occurs as a consequence of the
inhumanity of nature, its random violence and cruelty.
Depression, schizophrenia, paranoia, mania, obsessive
compulsive disorders, panic disorders, infertility are all
expressions of nature whose primary treatment must be
by nature, at the hands of physicians and psychiatrists
and through medications.

Specific counseling "postures" or "turns in the conversation" correspond to each of these levels of disorder.

When a client is clearly struggling in a total vacuum
of self-knowledge, in addition to structuring sessions
around a "feeling journal," I encourage ventilation—just
pouring it out, just talking, and talking, and talking,
telling me the events of the day or week, what moved
or didn't move them, until "something comes up"—a
feeling or desire "worth talking more about." Or I keep
talking about my own experience, or clients I remember
who were "struggling just like you," "or feeling what I
suspect to be something very similar" although "it took
a long time for them to realize it," while encouraging
the client to "stop me before I use up the whole time," or
"when something leaps out at you that you want to say

more about." The purpose is desire and feeling identification, and integration.

I also encourage "experiments" with new behaviors and communications during the intervals between sessions, as in "This week I'm going to ask you to go ahead and try . . . And as you're doing it please try and take note of what comes into your mind at that moment—whether it's a feeling, a new thought, an image, some memory, I don't know, but afterwards, if you will, write it down, and try to talk to yourself more about it. It will give us something to talk about next week. Even if nothing comes or it doesn't work, we'll need to talk about that. It's just an experiment so we can get to know more about what is going on for you." Again, the goal is "growth in the spirit" or the self-knowledge that comes from knowing and claiming the truth about one's own desires and feelings.

Where the truth is known and claimed but doesn't alone set you free because you still don't know what to do or how to go about doing it, the talk turns to information, specific plans, skills and social skills training.

And if knowing what to do, a client still lacks the courage or will to do it, the talk becomes motivational, the counselor becomes motivator, inspirer, story teller, example, in the way that he responds to the "problems" that emerge in therapy, encourager, in the sense of Alfred Adler, or an "externalizer" in the sense of Michael White's technique for "externalizing" a problem or difficulty, so that we can get to know it better or understand what it wants.

A word more about inspiration.

When we describe something as "inspiring" we usually mean one of two things. First, we "inspire" through the example of our conduct, as in the leader who charges over the hill, the martyr who sacrifices her life, or the Saint who models holiness, may be said to "inspire" others to imitate her.

Second, by "inspiration" we identify a soaring speech or sermon that exercises a mysterious, but visible or palpable exemplary effect on its listeners so that it "inspires" them to action, effort or change.

Both senses translate to therapy. In counseling the therapist can "inspire" a client through the example of his attitude and behavior within the session—the courage with which she faces tension, unflattering truths, or difficult moments, the compassion, patience, grace and understanding that she demonstrates or—

She can inspire by presenting images, ideals, interpretations, positive connotations, noble ascriptions, as the family therapists say, in which a client is able to glimpse his "higher self," or the better angel of his nature, with such clarity and intensity, that, in his surprise or astonishment at its appeal and potential realization, it ignites both his desire to be it, or a mild shame that he is not yet it.

In his novel *Home From the Hill*, William Humphrey provides, through the mouth of one of his characters, a description of just this sort of "inspiring" effect:

He told us stories about ourselves, stories in
which we were heroes, most often things we
ourselves had long ago forgotten and never
had seen much heroic in; but listening to him
tell it over, with his dark, humorless, intense
young face, you got the feeling that you *had*
looked pretty good on that occasion, and that
it *was* something memorable. It was a little
like reading about yourself in a book, in old-
fashioned and formal language full of words
that amused and yet pleased and at the same
time embarrassed you a little just because they
both amused and pleased, words like *courageous, valiant*, even *fortitude*, even *steadfast*,
words he got from his reading in Scott, Marryat,
Cooper, and Southern historians of The Lost
Cause. When he told you of a time when you
had been more courageous, more loyal, more
valiant than you knew perfectly well you ever
had been, it shamed you into resolving to live
up to his notion of you in the future . . . You did
not want to say or do anything that would hurt
his regard for you or the fresh regard he had
given you for yourself.

Incidentally, this sort of inspiration is the traditional
function of the bard in his "praise poems," which to us,
read at several or more centuries removed from their
source, often seem stilted set pieces of shameless syco-
phancy in flattery of princes and nobility hardly deserving of such praise. But the purpose of the praise poem,
like the purpose of inspiration in counseling through
whatever means, is to inspire its subject to a more worthy and exalted life.

Where motivation and inspiration fail because "rational-izations" or "defenses" reinforce them, the counselor's role changes to that of "a break-out man" in the sense of helping people break out of their own self-imposed prisons. The counselor becomes the lead conspirator in constant conspiratorial talk aimed at how we gonna break you out of here? How you gonna get better? How we gonna defuse and disarm those defenses, those iron bars that do a prison make?

My style is to usually do this through humorous exaggeration, as for instance "and you do that and you'll have to go in the desert and die" in response to "catastrophizing" or "Help me out here, sometimes I'm not too bright, but it seems inconsistent to me when you say you think this, but your experience, at least as you've described it, doesn't fit the interpretation," or "I'm sorry, but you're going to have to talk to me like a two-year-old who can't understand very much unless you talk slow, and are very, very specific and concrete when you tell me something" in response to abstractions or over-generalizations, or "Do you think it would be harder to do that, or count to ten without thinking about rabbits?" or "Learning how to walk?" to a client who is overestimating.

To overcome avoidance I often use a form of paradoxical intervention by encouraging a client "to just go on avoiding that, 'cause I don't want you to have too much fun, and I got plenty of more interesting things I'd rather talk about, and I hate to see somebody getting better before I'm through talking about it." Sometimes I just try to put the beast to sleep by talking about it so much that the client gets tired of me talking about it and decides to shut me up by just doing it. I call it "beating a dead horse long enough until it gets up and walks."

But, most typically, I try to defuse, dissolve, and disarm defenses, by just asking clients what the better part of them, "the soul or the spirit in you, thinks about this and are you keeping faith with it? Keeping the faith, doing what you know it's gonna take to let your spirit rise. Ever heard that song, 'I will rise, I will rise, I will rise?' Well, you better start rising, or I'm gonna start singing it to you, every session. And I got faith in you—I've seen that spirit shining in you, speaking in you. Now go out this week, goddamm it, and let your spirit rise. Don't let the man get you. It's too many of us— Rise."

"Don't let the man get you. Don't let him do what he done to me." That's a line from my other great rock-and-roll passion, John Fogerty. A line that both inspires, and helps to overcome defenses especially when their spiritually hurtful and diminishing impact has been recognized.

And I not only try to defuse defenses, I identify and encourage talk about them: "What other ways, and how else do you see this kind of thing holding you back— holding you back from the person you can be, that's in there in you like a spirit ready to flex its wings, a child of God, being the person God made you to be, wants to be, keeping the faith with the idea that God had when he made you? You know that's what Isak Dineson—you know the movie *Out of Africa*, that's her and about her—that's what she said pride is: keeping faith with the idea God had when She made you. For Christ's sake, get some pride and get going."

And finally, building on this last statement, I sometimes just encourage a client to just say to heck with their defenses. "Just treat them sort of like a quarterback treats his offensive lineman: they're big, they're often ugly, but they're there for a reason if you will just use them in the way they're meant to be used, which is to protect you when you need them, and to line up in front of you—your goal, your desire, your higher Self, and clear everything and every one else out of the way. The problem is not with generalization, or catastrophizing, or overestimating, or avoidance, or projection, etc., the problem is when they harm instead of help you to become who you truly are."

The overarching purpose of all this remains, from the point of view of the therapeutic session, to make the session's talk as productive, as educational and healing, as informational, cathartic, inspiring, humorous, strengthening, encouraging, memorable and the least interrupted, distracted, or ruined by the intrusion of blocks and defenses, and perhaps, as politically aware and committed, as possible, so that the "man" don't get none of us.

Now, the political statement:

Romantics are often criticized for their assumption that human suffering and unhappiness are caused, or largely so, by the evils of corrupt institutions or economic orders—Blake's "dark satanic mills."

With the one proviso that I do believe, as do most of those in the Romantic tradition (read even the despair of the later Shelley, for example, in his "Triumph of Life") that nature, while not evil, is randomly destructive, including the final tragedies of age, disease, and death. I do not shrink away from my already-stated credo that human nature is fundamentally good, or minimally, desirous of good, of being good, and that it is institutions and the socioeconomic order that corrupts us, both through its external afflictions and through the mechanisms of self-misery that it introduces into us.

And, today there really is bad moon rising.

For decades James Hillman grumbled about the fact we've had a hundred years of solitude in psychotherapy while the world is getting worse. He's right. We have. It is.

There is really a rough beast slouching, or as Van Morrison says, alluding to Yeats, "a rough god gliding" in contemporary culture, and to acknowledge it, the discord and the ills, the desert shadows and glacial chills, may more acutely sensitize us as therapists.

There are many ways to talk about this rough god. But being a Scotch-Irish Southerner, whose old country is Scotland and whose new country is the American South, I follow Faulkner in his conviction that what crippled the South as much as slavery, indeed made slavery possible, was what the sociologists call Calvinism.

We inhabit a landscape shackled by the chains of terrible old John Knox, the Scottish high priest of Calvinism, and with Calvin, a world grown comfortable, but mean and graceless, with the Calvinistic doctrines that repudiate the transcendent value of the feminine, reduce nature to raw materials and lifeless meaninglessness, and, most insidiously, the doctrine that riches and plenty prove virtue; that material, economic success confirms that one belongs to God's elect.

For psychotherapy, the Calvinist reduction of nature to raw materials is particularly negating. If nature is without value, so is human nature, which means that the call to self-knowledge, and the exploration of self that occurs in counseling is ultimately a waste of time. The old Catholic teaching is that nature is neither divine nor is it meaningless; rather it is a second order of revelation coexisting with the revelation that occurs directly through history from God to humanity. This would imply that self-knowledge and self-exploration, the philosophy, psychology, and anthropology of humanity, can be and perhaps ought to be pursued because in teaching us about our own human nature it also teaches us about God. Just as God calls us to know and experience Her through the Church and the Sacraments, She calls us to know Her through the contemplation of nature and meditation on ourselves.

For a Calvinist, psychotherapy is likely to seem like a waste of time, a meaningless self-pitying bout of navel-gazing, that if it were done, as Lady Macbeth says about the murder of Duncan, High King of Scotland, "it were well that it be done quickly" and secretly.

A Catholic might or really should see counseling as one
road for contemplating, through work on oneself, the
beauty, unity, and goodness of Divine Love.

This concern about "who's the true enemy?" warrants
an additional comment. Catholic theologians and politically conservative Catholic lay people often mistake, I
think, the real danger to Catholic religion and culture.
They think it's the New Age. They worry about the
explicit paganism of New Age spiritually while embrac-
ing, without thought or reservation, the fundamental
tenets of Calvinism, which they make the cornerstone
of their personal morality and successful careers. New
Age ideas are in some ways in opposition to the Catholic
way of life. But it's not nearly so dangerous as Calvinism, which is itself only a later version of Manichaeism,
with its condemnation of almost everything associated
with mortality, matter, the feminine, and the earth. The
Catholic Church, with its "worship" of Mary, our "idols,"
mysterious rituals and rites, the whole "puddle of pa-
pistry," as John Knox so temperately called it, are often
thought by other Christians to be one step removed from
paganism itself.

The strength of Catholicism has always been its ability
to assimilate and adapt what it finds valuable in diverse
traditions. As Greeley writes:

> The "sacramentalism" of the Catholic heritage
> has also led it to absorb as much as it thinks
> it can from what it finds to be good, true, and
> beautiful in pagan religions: Brigid is converted
> from pagan goddess to the Christian patron of
> spring, poetry, and new life in Ireland; Guadalupe

is first a pagan and then a Christian shrine in
Spain and then our Lady of Guadalupe becomes
the patron of poor Mexicans. This "baptism" of
pagan metaphors (sometimes done more wisely
than at other times) adds yet another overlay of
stories to the Catholic heritage.

No, the real enemy to the Catholic heritage is Calvinism. Frankly, I feel much more at home in a New Age
bookstore, with its incense, images, celebration of
the feminine and gentle spirituality than I would at a
gathering of Promise Keepers. In the first I feel something akin of what a Medieval Catholic might have
felt making an obeisance "just for luck" to an ancient
shrine; while about the second I can't help but see
the ghosts of Calvin, Knox, and Cromwell rising and
remembering that it wasn't so many centuries ago that
such rallies were likely to end with the crowd stream-
ing out to burn a priest or two at the stake, and behead
a King if it could find one. My authority for seeing far
more danger in the fundamentalist Christian Right than
in any civilized or Platonizing pagan or New Ager, are
the Greek fathers and St. Augustine who reviled Manichaeism in any form, but who held the Platonists and
other pagan philosophers in high regard and frequently
drew from them. Von Balthasar certainly finds a place
in his "symphony of truth" for the "gods," whether in
Greek mythology, Goethe, or Heidegger, and for pan-
theism, which he calls "the most positive attainable
conception of natural, philosophic religion and mysticism" in its "infinite recognition and trust manifested
toward the maternal-protective power of nature, and
toward the mystery of the ground of Being." *(Glory of
the Lord, I, 94.)*

These Calvinist doctrines are drab, but very noisy, wide-spread core ideas into which we all are socialized and indoctrinated by means too subtle to ever exhaustively map or grasp.

I once heard the director Louis Malle respond to a question about his film *Murmurs of the Heart*, a story about incest between a son and mother that has a happy ending; that is, incest turns out to be healing and renewing. Malle explained that wherever there was genuine human emotion, human trust, vulnerability and love, he was all sympathy and understanding. But for that cold, hard, mean pettiness—that better than and get the best of your neighbor attitude that afflicts so many now—he could feel only revulsion and contempt.

But a therapist is what I am, a livelihood that I share with most of you who are reading this essay. So it's all I can do to talk with some sophistication, and with luck, clairvoyance, about psychotherapy. But the way therapy happens in my office, and the symbols and fidelities through which I conceive and practice it, belong to a politics of hope—a politics of family over factory farm; of sticking to the union; of labor over capital; Main Street over Wall Street; of small town, downtown over Wal-Mart on the highway; of individually and locally owned businesses over chains and corporate behemoths; of human and civil rights, especially children's rights over free trade, over the resurgent Calvinism of "end of history" market ideologues; of the return of public shame and shunning of greed; of producer over marketer; of a tax on advertising budgets; of the relief and second chance of liberal bankruptcy laws that at least impose some

risk on usury; of homestead exemptions; of real doctors
over managed care; of the mutual obligations between
employer and employee; of education and health care
access for all; of economics reclaimed by morality; of
recognition that every purchase of goods or services is a
moral act, so that when in order to save a few pennies or
show off our status we choose the chain or multination-
al over our neighbor's chance for ownership, or a decent,
dignified livelihood; then it were better if a millstone had
been tied around our neck—a green, agrarian, distribu-
tivist, feudalistic, Cavalier, Young Englander, Red Tory;
a Southern, Celtic, Christian, Catholic politics of hope
that in the future, through revulsion from the squalor
of greed and spread of ugliness, a nostalgia for beauty
through the preservation of the earth; a demand for a
human growth-based economy; a chivalrous defense of
the poor, the old, the abandoned, and the needy; and the
miracle of grace we in unison will do eventually what
the beautiful Catholic Queen of Scotland, Mary Stuart,
the archetype perhaps, but certainly earlier version of
Princess Diana, could not—that is, defeat John Knox and
Calvin, their depredations, their despicable spoliations,
the damning and demeaning inhumanity of their legacy.

Freedom. *Freedom*. I practice humanistic counseling as a
freedom song.

I think the core issue of counseling in the 21st century
will be freedom. Perhaps Kierkegaard and Heidegger
can serve as guides in this new century, the way they
did at its midpoint of the last. And St. Augustine—the
first existentialist, and in the eyes of M. H. Abrams
in his masterpiece *Natural Supernaturalism*, the first

Romantic. Freedom, as St. Augustine understood it—St. Augustine who although almost fatalistic in attitude, overwhelmed by external chaos, ruin, and despair, and by the opacity and complexity of consciousness, and at times, the near absence of God, nevertheless refused to despair about freedom. For St. Augustine the soul was always free, on some level, and in some way, although it could be difficult to discern this.

I think the theme of 21st century psychotherapy will emerge as the struggle to help clients find within themselves that sliver of light, that barely burning sputtering candle, nearly engulfed by the blackness and weight of over generalizations, of catastrophizing, so that they can begin to exercise their freedom, to choose what they want to do, and then do it. This often requires redefining problems and goals so that they become identifiable, step by identifiable step, resolvable and reachable, but the will to do it still requires the exercise of freedom.

Let me instance this. A client comes in. She is in her thirties, exceptionally bright, verbal. She is married to a businessman as upwardly mobile as a flame in a wind tunnel. Her issues are multiple depression—she cries all the time, is becoming progressively isolated and unhappy.

Her husband is angry, their sex life almost nonexistent. Further conversation indicates that the root of his anger is the state of the apartment. Even further conversation, that begins to take on the flooding intensity of a confession, reveals the state to be "awful." She never cleans house: dirty dishes everywhere, bathrooms uncleaned, beds never made, clothes heaped up, etc. Because of the mess, it's too embarrassing to have people over. She lives in fear that someone will drop in. The husband is beginning to stay away, she thinks to avoid both her and the mess.

"Could you get a maid?" I wonder.

"Too expensive," she says.

"Cheaper than divorce."

"It's a power thing with him. He's just not going to do it," she responds.

"I wonder what would happen if you just said, 'To hell with that, I'm getting a maid'?"

"No," she smiles through the tears.

"Do you have your own money or checkbook? Is there no way to just do it, and he can deal with the aftermath, which, I guess would be a clean house anyway."

"No," the smile is lingering.

"Tell you what you do. You fix him a great dinner, wine, flowers, etc. Clear a path to the bedroom. Wear something seductive. Then play him Muddy Waters doing "I Just Want to Make Love to You"—you know that one with the lyrics "I don't want you . . . " well, basically sings about not wanting his lady to waste her time cleaning, he just wants to make love to her. Possible?"

The smile becomes a grin.

"Look, what it comes down to is this. I think you ought to get a maid, or put your foot down with your husband and tell him he's gonna help. Or you're gonna have to do it yourself. I know it seems impossible now when you think about it. Maybe you could get a maid or a cleaning service to come in once, and then you can work on it a little bit every day—pick your time, maybe just a half an hour or an hour, one room a day, or maybe your husband would agree to divvy up the cleaning chores, or maybe the two of you could take one week and really clean house for a weekend, and then reward yourself with a romantic weekend getaway—but what it all comes down to, with any of these things, is you—

Your freedom.

"The question is, 'Is this something you can't do, or you won't do?' If you really think you can't get this house clean, that there's something in you that needs it this way, then we need to start thinking about depression, compulsive disorder, these are biochemical things, brain dysfunctions and we need to get you to a psychiatrist to have you evaluated for medication which will help.

"But if it's you can, but you won't, then you need to find that place within, where despite everything you feel is overwhelming you, hurting you way down deep, you're still free, a human being, special, worthwhile, deserving, a child of God, and from that space you need to choose to get this house cleaned up one way or another. If you don't, it's going to continue to make you unhappy and my guess is that even if your husband loves you beyond words, it's going to kill your marriage.

"I'm going to stop today, reminding you that you are a beautiful soul and a worthwhile human being, and you've got the grand gift of human freedom in you, freedom to struggle and risk to make your life better. I'm betting this week that you're gonna get in touch with that and change your life. And I'm going to try and reach your husband to tell him exactly the same thing too—he's as free and responsible for the house as you are."

Let me acknowledge as we head for the bunkhouse, that critiques have been made of the idea of counseling as essentially a "talk," for example, in criticism of Glasser's reality therapy, where therapy is defined as essentially a "conversation." Reality therapy, like most psychotherapies, is a *conversation* between a therapist and a client or clients. Arnold Lazarus argues that a viable science of psychotherapy needs more than "conversation" and often demands specific techniques that have empirical backing. Also needed are treatment outcomes that supply precise specifications beyond a vague allusion to something called "helpfulness."

Now there's a whole nest of assumptions tucked up under the floorboards of this critique, most of which originate in the "correspondence" definition of truth, that is, truth is an abstract picture or formulation in the mind that "matches" or corresponds to an external, objective reality, and is associated with the attitude of science. I leave it to the philosophers such as Husserl, Whitehead,

Heidegger, Merleau-Ponty, Polanyi, E. A. Burtt, etc. to criticize and relativize these assumptions.

My aggressive retort relies just on the at-hand, common-sense, look-there evidence that although words such as "scientific," "empirical," and "precise specifications" are very impressive sounding, and likely to intimidate everyone in the room who had trouble with, or even bailed out of the clinical psychology curriculum because they couldn't master statistics, the fact is that the one undeniable fact about psychotherapy is that it is and will remain, if nothing else, a talking cure, unless that is, Dr. Lazarus is proposing some new form of a scientific, abstract, logical, wordless form of healing. I think we get farthest by simply sticking with that, and developing and attempting to illuminate from the phenomena of counseling ideas and methods to understand, determine and maximize its efficacy.

In other words, let the truth about counseling unfold and reveal itself within the phenomena of counseling, as opposed to imposing ideas or methods derived elsewhere from theory or research which are assumed to "match" the reality "behind" or "underlying" the phenomena, in an attempt to explain, control, or predict it.

And, then, in closing, let me acknowledge some kinship with "Narrative Therapy." Some kinship, but not much. On narrative therapy's own grounds I would distinguish between our respective approaches in terms of the Burkean genre idea. Where I'm romantic to the core, narrative therapy and indeed most of its immediate forebears all the way back to Erickson, are "comic" in meaning and approach. It's the comic universe that Erickson inhabited and into which, like some desert Prospero managing his stage, his Ariel and Caliban, he introduced his "shipwrecked" clients.

But there is more, a difference too profound to be negotiated. You see, I'm a realist. I believe in truth. Narrative therapists—if I read them rightly and understand correctly that their approach rests upon constructivist and de-constructivist philosophy—don't. They don't believe in truth. But phenomenological existentialism, spiritual existentialism does. Heidegger and von Balthasar quest for truth. Counseling, with me, is a romance of truth experienced through language, not a "management" of conversation.

The last responsibility, and finally, the most meaningful, that I would impose upon the counselor, is that he or she care for truth, so that the more adaptive and creative therapeutic conversation that is internalized by the client, with which he engages, identifies, and assimilates, is also quickened by a deep concern for truth.

Therapeutic conversation is a dramatic engagement in quest of truth, rather than, as with narrative therapy, a manipulative or exploratory or "creatively playful" operation or maneuver whose objectives are simple and elegant solutions to life and family problems.

Truth. Truth is the music. The music. "Truth is symphonic," said von Balthasar. Truth is the King's Great Horn, the spiritual ditty of no tone. Truth is the music—and talk—talk is the dance, the vehicle by which we

most passionately and seductively experience the music
and go deeper into it. The therapist is the first to hit the
dance floor, the one who leads, and through his rhythm
and movement draws another deeper into the music, to
a new and transforming experience of it, that gradually
ripens and matures into a new individual expression.

Talk to me. Talk to me. Talk to me. But tell me the truth,
the whole truth and nothing but the truth, so help you
God. And I will tell you the truth about me. I know it's
the truth that will set us free.

May I offer one last image of conversation?

> Cockran . . . cut a remarkable figure, tower-
> ing, leonine, with deep-set eyes and a massive
> forehead. His mobile features gave a contem-
> porary the impression of "something Spanish,
> Celtiberian as well as Celtic. His oratory was
> remarkable. Twice, in 1884, and 1892, his deep,
> resonant brogue had held Democratic national
> conventions spellbound. Churchill was to be one
> of his early conquests. Among the last was Adlai
> Stevenson, who modeled his own rhetoric on
> Cockran's. In the early 1950's Churchill would
> astound Stevenson by quoting long passages
> from Cockran speeches.
>
> . . . But there was no doubt about which New
> Yorker impressed him most. . . Night after night,
> long after Barnes had retired (Cockran and
> Churchill) sat in the flat's large library, sipping
> brandy, smoking cigars—Churchill's first—and
> talking, talking, talking . . . Churchill was en-
> thralled by his host's fire, vision, vigor, and most

of all, by his own mastery of English. (William Manchester, *The Last Lion: Winston Churchill, Visions of Glory, 1874-1932*,Boston: Little Brown and Company, 1983, pp. 222-226.)

Bourke Cockran, a truly "generative" conversationalist whose talk profoundly influenced, indeed was formative for, two of the greatest men of their century.

Freedom. A freedom song. Freedom of expression. A freedom rediscovered and reexperienced through a conversation, through the crack, through dialogue, through talking something through.

The *Way* of Spiritual Existential Counseling

May I end with a prayer? Two prayers really, to unite and celebrate my Southern, Celtic, Catholic heritage, grits, scones, and wine and bread—

The first is known as St. Patrick's Breastplate, or "The Deer's Cry" because it was said that in the eyes of his enemies, the Saint would suddenly be transformed into a deer when he recited this prayer.

I try to say it every day in preparation for my work, it together with one of the Psalms.

> I arise today Through the strength of heaven: Light of sun, Radiance of moon, Splendor of fire, Speed of lightning, Swiftness of wind, Depth of sea, Stability of earth, Firmness of rock.
>
> I arise today Through God's strength to pilot me: God's might to uphold me. God's wisdom to guide me, God's ear to hear me, God's word to speak for me, God's hand to guard me, God's way to live before me, God's shield to protect me, God's host to save me From snares of devils, From temptation of vices, From everyone who wishes me ill Afar and anear, Alone and in a multitude.
>
> Christ to shield me today Against poison, against burning, Against drowning, against wounding, So that there may come to me abundance of reward. Christ with me, Christ before me, Christ behind

me, Christ in me, Christ beneath me, Christ above
me, Christ on my right hand, Christ on my left,
Christ when I lie down, Christ when I sit down,
Christ when I arise, Christ in the heart of every
man who thinks of me, Christ in the mouth of
everyone who speaks of me, Christ in every eye
that sees me, Christ in every ear that hears me.

I arise today Through the almighty strength, the
invocation of the Trinity: Through a belief in the
Threeness, Through confession of the Oneness Of
the Creator of Creation.

Then, in response, as one verse or song, as Hillman
says, might lead to another, my own prayer-poem,
Wildflower Christian—

I believe in a kind of East Texas Christ, a Christ of
red dirt and cattle grazing at dusk.

A Christ who after summer drought, autumn sun-
shine, winter frost, springtime rains, bursts like a
wildflower in the heart.

I believe in a Christ who was born of an un-
wed mother, who was a teenage runaway, who
brought wine to the party, who cooked fish for
his friends.

And when he did, I'm betting it was catfish, fried
fillets heaped high from behind a school cafeteria counter, baked beans, cole slaw swimming in
mayonnaise and vinegar, Mrs. Baird's bread. A
Friday night fund-raiser probably for the school
or Church—or maybe it was on a creek bank, in a

black skillet on an open mesquite fire, beneath a tall
overhanging tree, the thick fragrant smoke rising
and curling through the branches, stars out, a falling star plunging down to the water, children laugh-
ing, adult faces raw with the sun and worry washed
clean and innocent by the moonlight, the sky itself a
milky blue-dark sparkle, fireflies dipping, flickering,
mosquitos whining, the creek water shining and
gurgling as it rushes over slick, white, green mossy
veined stones.

Christ—Christ before me, Christ beneath me, as
the prayer of St. Patrick says.

St. Patrick, St. Francis, Friar Tuck, a red dirt, wildflower and catfish Christ.

I believe in a Christ who liked to walk through
the cornfields on Sunday, who had the strength
to draw up a big heavy bucket of foaming water
from a deep country well.

A Christ who picked his disciples from the guys in
the gimme caps, fishing underneath the highways,
knees deep in the mist on Easter morning, and—

From the women who may have married or slept
with too many guys, but who raise their kids decent, take the old to the doctor, stay close to their
family and friends.

And one of them washed Christ's feet—was it a
nurse or teacher's aid? A waitress, maybe on her
feet all day or standing behind a cash register all
night, too old, too weary to do this kind of work,

but needs the money and knows that sore feet in
a hot tub of Epsom salt is about as close to pure
bliss as you can get, if you're still walking that
dusty back road to paradise?

A Christ whose hands were calloused and rough
enough to dig a post hole and stretch barbed wire,
but gentle, oh so gentle, to ease, in the muck and
the mire, an hour before dawn, a turned wrong
calf down the birth canal and then watch the cow
lick it clean, fresh coat streaked like Joseph's in
the sunrise.

A gentle Christ, a healing Christ, but a Christ who
would roar with rage.

A Christ who sprinkled his parables with a dew-
fall of poetry about birds in the air and lilies in
the field.

A rural small-town Christ who knows when
you're sick and cares when you die.

And when you're too old, sick, too full of grief
or loneliness to cook, shows up with a basket
filled with supper, iced tea in jars wrapped in red
checkered napkins to keep it cool, and then sits
awhile, on the front porch in the cool of the evening, the ambling meaningless conversation like
a quietly murmured prayer and then stays late to
wash the dishes.

Red brick town Church, roadside Pentecostal,
Catholic Mission to the poor.

A honeysuckle gospel—built upon joy in who we are—tolerance and laughter, humor and healing, —and love.

The yoke is easy, the burden is light.

Appendix One

Seeing Red: A Tribute to
James Hillman

*My first piece of fiction, published in 1950, climaxes in
a bullfight.*

—James Hillman, Preface, Volume 9, UE

Seeing red: that's what James Hillman has meant for me.
Seeing red: the outrage that gave rise to his best thinking, a martial thinker, a child of Mars, the angry red
planet, Holst's Mars "the most devastating piece of music
ever written" it's been called, Strife is all, War is all,
Nature as a Heraclitian fire, the Thought of the Heart—
"Imagination is born in the blood not in the dreaming
psyche," he said that already in *The Myth of Analysis*,
the Lion Roaring at the Desert, Mars, Mithras, St. Michael, the bellowing bull, the bull in the China Shop of
Jungian Psychology, Imagination is Bull . . .

Let me conjure here with Cormac McCarthy (McCarthy
moved to Texas about the same time as Hillman. Mc-
Carthy moved to El Paso, which he called "one of the last
real cities in America" where he ate every night at Lu-
by's. Hillman favored the Highland Park Cafeteria). The
magnificent passage that perorates the first book of the
Trilogy, John Grady Cole, coming back to where?—coming back to Texas: do you remember it: the red desert,
the red dust, the blood-red sunset and the solitary bull

"rolling against the dust . . . like an animal in sacrificial torment . . . "?

Coming back to Texas: Seeing red: the evening redness in the West, seeing red, red dirt, red neck, red state, a red granite capitol, red King Ranch Santa Gertrudis cattle, first new breed in the new world, blood-red sunset and Comanche moon, red Comanche riding down what's now I-35 all the way to the Gulf, "when you cross that old Red River boy / it just don't mean a thing / it don't matter who's in Nashville / Bob Wills is still the King."

Seeing red. Seeing red. But it was always there implicitly, incipiently. It is there in this book, this Volume I; it was there in Hillman's first book, *Emotion.* Dick Russell quotes Ed Casey as saying how different *Emotion* appears in light of his subsequent writing. "It has a lot of system," said Casey, "and structure that is no longer the case even three or four years later with his other writings." I propose the opposite: *Emotion*, as are these essays collected in Volume I (and why it is so fitting that the *Uniform Edition* begins this way), is the foundation of his work, the that without which, the *sine qua non*, Hillman, in my view, can be neither understood nor recognized as the *sui generis* genius that he was.

And, I might add why, again, in my view, he fit at the University of Dallas and why he left there, here—restless, disappointed, angry, perhaps, justifiably so, at UD's obtuseness—but, nonetheless, re-oriented in outlook. It was here that he made his now-renowned "turn to the world" in a manner reminiscent of St. Thomas in the 13th Century in response to the re-discovery of Aristotle. Maybe it was phenomenology, Merleau-Ponty or the Munich School; maybe it was Faulkner and Dostoevsky; maybe it was Ransom, Tate, and Warren; maybe it was the influence of Thomism that really was in the air then, a distillate, breathed in breathed out, alive and well and living on campus, at the Dominican Priory whose priests taught the theology classes nine hours of which were required of every undergraduate student. Maybe it was what Belloc called the "Catholic Thing," saturated as it is in worldliness and the appeal to the senses. Maybe, and, most likely, it was the cultural desert that Dallas must have seemed to him, provoking the Lion's roar, the thought of the heart. Whatever it was, Hillman left Dallas with an enhanced, and very Thomistic, even Hopkins-like, sense of what John Crowe Ransom called the World's Body: *"plow down sillion shine, and blue bleak embers. Ah, my dear, fall and gall themselves and gash gold vermillion."*

UD, when I got there, which was as a summer student, in 1969, *was* a Medieval University. You'll have to take my word for it, or, you really had to be there. Marshall McLuhan, who admired the Middles Ages and thought they were re-appearing, was, for awhile. In a letter to a friend written a few months after Hillman first visited in 1975, McLuhan described UD as "an ideal learning environment." It was certainly one of the few Universities in the 70s where students got into drunken fist fights, not over girls or politics, but over fine points in Medieval philosophy. College as Scarborough Fair. Everywhere a song and a celebration. Medieval Times had returned to other universities during that era—the Woodstock Nation and a children's crusade to change the world. But instead

of the SDS and the Weathermen, we had the Sons of
Thunder, Catholic Restorationists, in khaki and red be-
rets, shouting *Viva Christo Rey*! *Hispanidad*, a half-cen-
tury too soon. The University of Dallas *must* have been
the only University anywhere in the world at the time,
where one could study both Thomism, with Sir Frederick
Wilhelmsen, one of the great existential Thomists of the
last century, and alchemy and neo-Platonism with James
Hillman. Only at a Medieval University could that by any
stretch seem normal. It did at UD.

I will not quite maintain that Hillman was a medieval
thinker—but Medieval / Renaissance shade into each
other in countless ways—what fuses them is that they
antedated the Reformation, the Scientific Revolution,
Modernity and the disenchantment of the world—but
the key to his work and the reason that *Emotion* and the
essays collected in Volume I of the Uniform Edition are
so essential to a full appreciation of it—the magnificence,
the scope, the subtlety, the volume, the virtuosity, the
depth, the bulk, the reach, is that Hillman's work consists—I would argue—of a lifelong practice of a form of
thought and expression known in the thirteenth century,
while also providing its intellectual life blood, as *disputatio*. Emotion explicitly takes this form. The *disputatio*
is an agonistic form. *Disputatio* is seeing red. It is the
corrida, the bullfight. It is dancing not on a pin head
but on the horns of a dilemma. It is Cretan bull leaping
as mental gymnastic: *So now they come back! Hark! /
Hark! the low and shattering laughter of bearded men
/ with the slim waists of warriors, and the long feet /
of moon-lit dancers. / Oh, and their faces scarlet, like
the dolphin's blood! / Lo! the loveliest is red all over,*

rippling vermilion, that's Lawrence—*The Heroes Are Dipped in Scarlet*. It is the bull sublimated. It is the Bull Sublime. In a *disputatio* one proceeds, like the bullfight, through disciplined opposition: one raises a question, as in "What is Emotion?" or "Why Archetypal Psychology?" establishes the method; assembles all the theories and arguments and does so exhaustively; considers them; presents them; then states one's own position; refutes, answers, legitimates, and integrates, when possible, conflicting views. *Disputatio* ultimately achieves its goal through synthesis, which,—speaking of St. Thomas—is the human mind's analogical participation in the act that existence is, the issing that synthesizes disparate essences into the uniqueness—again, Hopkins, the haecceity, the eachness, of individual things. This is the structure of *Emotion* and, also, to large extent, of the essays collected in Volume I. Works engendered in this way are irreducibly individual; their uniqueness mirrors the uniqueness of things, together with their stubborn opacity and autonomy.

As a fundamental form of thought, of intellectual development, I don't think Hillman ever much departed from the spirit, if not, the letter, of the *disputatio*. In some works, it imparts a kind of formalism and schematic nature to the presentation which, to some, like Dr. Casey, seem a departure from Hillman's more errant and enticing efforts. I beg to differ. I think his work, from start to finish, *coheres*. It was / is a lifelong *disputatio* whose one goal is to make clear—vigorously, contentiously, even belligerently, but so precisely and, often, so, so beautifully, a matter of what Tillich called "ultimate concern," the matter being soul, the *logos*, the probing precisions

and differentiations of an acutely critical mind, the *logos
of the soul*, psychology. The *disputatio* fit his martial
temperament; substantiated his relish for exhaustive,
comprehensive scholarship; legitimized polemics and a
robust, agonistic style; excused excess and caricature at
times; and, most importantly, allowed for an astonish-
ing success at assimilative and regenerative synthesis.
Because he loved the old, and sometimes, seemed like he
knew everything—I once heard him quote Commander
Cody in a lecture—"the Armadillo Stomp" from their '74
classic *Live in the Deep Heart of Texas*—ransacked and
scavenged it, like a knight errant or a *bricoleur*, I suppose, but really more like a *berserker* Viking, he made so
many things new. Hillman overcame what Harold Bloom
called "the Anxiety of Influence." After reading Hillman, the psychologies of Freud, Jung and Adler, Murray
Bowen, Ivan Bozormenyi-Nagy, Minuchin, and Haley
seem branches of Archetypal Psychology, specialized
areas for investigating the soul of Sex, Self, Power, Family. The outcome of Hillman's practice of *disputatio* is an
extraordinary *sui generis* psychology—a psychology that
ultimately leaves nothing out; where everything is saved
and salvaged, everything valuable, useful, beautiful,
lofty, crooked, perverse, poignant, true. Nothing is left on
the table; everything belongs. Hillman had something to
say about everything. Nothing human was alien to him;
and everything he spoke of, because of that speaking,
became more humane, that is, *claimed*, as ineradicably,
and, from a Catholic point of view, redeemably, human.

Which leads me to my final statement: I mentioned recognition of what is most impressive and lasting in Hillman. It is the fact that he leaves nothing out. No matter

what you are thinking about, confronting as a therapist
or a patient or a citizen or a reader or a lover or a fighter,
or a philosopher or an artist, or tinker, tailor or candle-
stick maker, Hillman has something valuable to say to
you—often something so valuable that it shocks into a
new awareness—reading as a Zen slap or an electro-
shock treatment. The lifelong practice of *disputatio*, of an
agonistic, martial engagement with life—an engagement
splendid and fiery and abundantly creative—conferred a
richness on his work, a fullness, a plenitude, a kind of
roundness, as Delmore Schwarz exalted "roundness" in
one of his poems, as the Greek ideal, the *kalos kagathos*
is well rounded. Can I remind you of Werner Jaeger's
definition of the *kalos kagathos*? It is *"the chivalrous
ideal of the complete human personality, harmonious in
mind and body, foursquare in battle and speech, song
and action."* "Foursquare in battle and speech, song
and action"—a serviceable description of Hillman, the
psychologist, the man. It is this foursquare, mandala-
like richness that ultimately distinguishes his work and
renders it so satisfying, so satisfying that it does repay—repay, with an exponential multiplier—forty years
of reading it. George Bernard Shaw said something once
about Mozart that applies to Hillman: *"Mozart, like Praxiteles, Raphael, Molière, Shakespeare was no leader of a
new departure or founder of a school. (One cannot say
about him) here is an entirely new vein of musical art, of
which nobody ever dreamt before Mozart . . . Anybody
almost can make a beginning: the difficulty is to make
an end—to do what cannot be bettered . . . It is always
like that: Praxiteles, Raphael and Co. have great men for
their pioneers, and only fools for their followers."* You
can count me as one of those fools.

Appendix Two

James Hillman: Preserving the Honor of Psychology

James Hillman was a psychologist, one of the few who deserve the name, the one, my argument is, who deserves it the most. Psychology: the Soul's Speech. Simple enough. But not so simple, not so obvious, since the entire discipline abides almost in total ignorance of it. If only ignorance were bliss. But it's not bliss. It is horribly destructive. Spend an hour reading the very best in CBT—Cognitive-Behavioral Psychology, the model most in vogue today. Where is the soul, where is the person, where is empathy and intimate understanding, personal identification with the damaged, the lonely, the afflicted, the "there but for the Grace of God go I"? Spend a day in Family Court where the experts parade their infernal violations of the fragile, intimate, vulnerable, mysterious, uncomprehending self of childhood. "Is the heart still beating?" asked the great Catholic writer Georges Bernanos. "But the world's heart is always beating. That heart is childhood. Were it not for the scandal of childhood, avarice and cunning would have dried up the world in a century or so." Parenting? What is parenting? There is really no such thing. There is only being a Father or a Mother, giving the gift of one's Self in Love and in Example. The key to being a good Father or Mother?—Stand for something, believe in something and order your life forthwith according to its canons. Psychology as a science? With its arsenal of medications and measurements and medicalization of almost every human saga does it not do as much harm as good? And every human has a Saga, a story to tell. By their stories, ye shall know them. And by enriching that story, detailing and deepening it, through the method of amplification, which, is the method proper to psychology, the method that is also a therapy, the only real therapy that satisfies the soul, psychology could be maybe, just maybe, worthy of its name.

I say Hillman was a psychologist, one of the few who deserve the name. He spoke so compellingly of it, with all its dirt and drama, suffering and splendor. The soul— what is it? He told us. It is *the that which is*, not "the none greater than can be thought" of Anselm's famous proof of God. The soul is that which is—

Communicated in love, so it must speak as lovers do of passion, tenderness, of beauty, of the elements. *How do I love you, let me count the ways. I love thee like a summer's day*. Or *Thereupon my heart is driven wild / she stands before me as a living child.*

Has a religious concern, has intimations of immortality, glimmers, hints, it is Christ-haunted, Pan-haunted, a Piper at the Gates of Dawn, the twinkling of the May Queen, responds to shrine and story, ruins, graveyards, fables, myth.

Has a special relationship with Death, with the dead, "Deep in the earth, they hear" said Pindar, "half in love with easeful death," said Keats.

Transforms events into experiences: it slows the passage of time, like a Peckinpah or Ridley Scott shot of violence, it intensifies, throws into sharp relief, pricks like a needle, engulfs like a wave, expands like a fragrance—a scent of flowers, perhaps, or like the perfume she wore, the touch of his hand, the soft skin and radiant warmth of a body lying next to yours in bed.

Hillman told us what it is, the soul, and he spoke of it. He spoke of it, with such magnificent force, appeal, comprehensiveness, and clarity that he created a near-encyclopedic psychology worthy of, matched to, the famous lines of Tertullian—"*Step forth, o Soul, and give thy testimony*," an encyclopedic psychology that restores the soul to its proper place in the economy of being.

Now this can also be said, to a large extent of Jung, of course. And that's what undoubtedly attracted Hillman to him. But on this matter of absolute fidelity to the soul, Jung is surpassed by Hillman. Hillman honored psychology, honored his calling, passionately, daringly, unswervingly, always with courage and grace. *He never swerved.* Jung swerved, for whatever reasons, for good reason, perhaps. The Red Book stayed under wraps. Different time, different place, different needs and expediencies. In Jung and Jungian psychology experience is all too often replaced by theory; image, by concept; psychology by theology or even pseudo-science. Catholic theologians and mystics interested Jung, not so much Catholic writers. Hillman differs. Hillman did not swerve. His fidelity is always to psychology, never to mysticism, theology or science, always, above all, first and foremost, exclusively to the soul.

Hillman honored the soul on its own terms. Jung, finally, did not. What do I mean by honor? What I mean by it is a passionate, daring, unswerving commitment to an ideal that deploys itself as moral, physical, spiritual, and intellectual courage. In my own "differentiated" version of archetypal psychology, honor is the goal, the absolute. I believe in the regal in man, the "royal self" as construed by Aristotle and Aquinas; that our goal, our salvation, if you will, is God; that Virtue, service, sacrifice, and stewardship are our noblest activities and that Honor is our only absolute—the Honor of God, of our Families, Communities, Churches, our Children, our own personal Honor. The work of any psychologist is the effort to honor people in such a way as to encourage them to lay claim to their own honor, to the very best about themselves.

Honor has always occupied a hallowed place in the annals of the West; if only to be debated, rejected—"Honor is mere escutcheon," as Falstaff says, re-claimed, re-constituted, once again. And, it certainly occupies a central place in George Bernanos. For Bernanos, honor was a watchword, the fulcrum upon which the world should turn. "Few words," says Bernanos, "can resist the sleazy distortions that the politician, the ideologue, the banker, and the casuists successively practice on language . . . Honor is one of those words . . . We can argue endlessly about legality, rights, and justice itself, because, alas, it isn't always easy to draw the distinctions between the letter and the spirit. But honor is hard evidence. It binds both the old man and the child, both the poor man and the rich, both the scholar and the ignorant, and it even seems that the noblest animals aren't entirely devoid of it. Honor is the salt of the earth. The world needs honor. What the world lacks is honor . . . Honor is an absolute." To his massive study of Bernanos, von Balthasar attaches this motto of an old Spanish Noble Family: "To lose one's life for one's Honor / To lose one's Honor for one's Soul."

As a psychology of honor, archetypal psychology expands into Cultural Psychology. Not only persons, but things can reclaim their honor. We honor the soul of anyone, of anything, by asking—the soul, remember, is communicated in love, connected to death, with a religious concern, transforms events into experiences: by asking, how can it be loved?; and, then, how is it mortal, "half in love with easeful death," limited, incomplete, shadowed by tragedy, brokenness and death, *memento mori*—psychology as a permanent *memento mori*, skull on the desks, blood for the ghosts, Mass on All Soul's Day in the cemetery, not the morbid fascinations of the Romantic Agony, but the realism and resolve of "Horseman, pass by," the Tragic Sense of Life?; and, what does any person, place or thing ask of us? Want of us? How does it stop us cold, dead in our tracks, arrest our motion?; where is the ember of hope, the reach of transcendence, the depths, the heights, the history? How can we abide with it, come to know what we love, the connections, the inter-connections. We must ask this of the pedophile and the concrete pavement as much as of myth, dreams, art, and literature. The devil is always in the details, so too the gods, so too the Saints and Heroes; so too is Christ. Phenomenology becomes archetypal psychology, a lyrical differentiating response to the Dead.

Another main difference separates Hillman from Jung. Jung's psychology typifies what Kathleen Raine called the

Great Tradition, "Occult" in the sense of Gilbert Durand: it is Protestant, German Romantic, Alchemical, Hermetic in the sense of Francis Yates, Gnostic.

In contrast—in near total contrast, in my view—Hillman's work belongs thoroughly to the mainstream of the Western tradition, the full flowering of which was first the Italian Renaissance, then, the French, finally, the English. In a classic essay Louise Cowan explains how it has always been the struggle of Christian culture to join Athens to Jerusalem, the Greek sense of form, their quest for beauty, their exaltation of reason, dialectic and logic, their enshrinement of the Polis, of *Arete* and competition with the Old Testament reality of prophetic utterance and gorgeous praise poetry—David danced before the Ark—irrupting thunderously, ecstatically amidst betrayal, alienation, suffering, and sin. *"Absalom, Absalom,"* the Golden Calf, the fiery bush. Tobit, a walk, not in the clouds, but through the desert, with an Angel. "One of the great strengths of Western Civilization has been its ability to produce artists and thinkers of sometimes outrageous paradox—witness such thinkers and artists as Augustine, Dante, El Greco, Donne, Milton, Goya, Beethoven, Goethe, Melville, Kierkegaard, Hopkins, Dostoevsky, Nietzsche, Mahler, Roualt and Faulkner, among others." Though, occasionally, I'll grant, he did sound that way; ultimately, and, as Paul Tillich taught us, nothing really matters other than "ultimate concerns," Hillman sups with these artists and thinkers not with Zen Master, Sufi poet, Hindu guru or Golden Chain of Wise Men. As he insisted time and time again, Hillman was Western in loyalty, heart, nerve, sinew.

Let me hang this argument on two threads, one slender, both strong. The first is via deconstructing not Hillman's texts, but his indexes. Start with A in *Revisioning Psychology*: Abenheimer, Abrams, Ackerknecht, Alberti, Albertus Magnus, Aleman, Allen, Allport, Ananke, Aphrodite, Apollo, Aquinas, Ares, Argan, Aristotle (thirteen entries, probably tops after Freud and Jung), Artemis, Asclepius, Athene, Auerbach, St. Augustine—eight entries. In another place I pointed out that in Hillman's final book, *A Terrible Love of War*, the entries under Patton outnumber those of Jung. These are names of Classicists, of Greek Gods, Christian Saints and Philosophers, Literary Critics, Psychologists. If by their indexes, ye shall know them, Hillman resembles Dante or Pound far more than Bruno, or, frankly, even Plotinus or Ficino.

Or take that most familiar, and, in many ways, most characteristic Hillman theme of the *Puer*. The theme, the image, is Greek of course, but it is also Judeo-Christian. It's David, perhaps—perhaps, quintessentially, David—the shepherd boy, the Warrior, the cup-bearer to a King, a cup-bearer who becomes a King—Saul has slain thousands, but David his tens of thousands. Here is the Glorious Doctor, Cardinal von Balthasar on the Christian: "The Christian has the privilege of remaining to the end, and in everything he does, a 'poet.' In the eyes of the children of this world he is a dreamer, not in the sense that he lacks the discipline of the Church and falls into childishness, but in the sense that he has a youthful enthusiasm for the model which he discovers and which he makes the idol of his heart. It is just at this point that the Word of God reveals his eternal, youthful power. He is youthful by nature; he does not simply put one into an enthusiastic mood, which will pass, He imparts substantially that Spirit that makes all things new. It is, inseparably, also the Spirit of Jesus who was always young . . . " For Bernanos the Saints—and the Saints, for Bernanos, are the Church, are forever young. "Our Catholic tradition, without harming them, sweeps them into the full flood of its universal rhythm. They are all there—St. Benedict with his raven, St. Francis with his lute and his Provençal songs, Jeanne with her sword, Vincent with his shabby *soutane*, and Teresa, the newcomer, so strange and hidden . . . smiling her incomprehensible smile." And Dominic, "where everything is pure, everything new, everything strives toward the heights, like the cosmic rising of the dawn . . . "

Speaking as a Catholic, a Christian, it is just here that we can understand the nature of Hillman's putative paganism and "attack upon Christendom" the aspect that so delights some, but so dismays and disturbs some Christians and Catholics. (A quick aside: when I worked for Spring Publications we brought out a new edition of David Miller's *The New Polytheism*. One afternoon we got a frantic call from the salesman with whom we dealt. The printer was owned and staffed by Evangelical Christians who were refusing to print the book. It was pagan. It took a lot of fast talking, explaining that we were not at all a Pagan Press; we were housed in fact at a Catholic University. That convinced them. Catholics, after all, are sort of Christians, and a bit of paganism mixed in was only to be expected.)

Hillman was not a pagan, nor is archetypal psychology. Instead, he was a deeply cultured, schooled, and appre-

ciative defender of the Classical Tradition. He once mused
to me that had he been alive during the Emperor Julian's
era, he would have probably become a Christian. As a
religion, the Greek and Roman pantheon was finished.
Archetypal Psychology is not theology. How many times
did he repeat this?

What archetypal psychology *is* is a Classical-Judeo-Chris-
tian psychology that speaks of, about, and to the soul,
that honors the soul, with its stories, its imagery, its
myths and legends, its fantasy, its emotion, its genius,
its darkness and its beauty, and in Hillman's hands it did
so with an inimitable eloquence and erudition.

The Catholic tradition is always in danger of losing its
soul, its culture, history, traditions, observances, the
"Catholic Thing" as Belloc called it. To Catholics such as
Bernanos, our modern Church can seem a very pallid
institution. We're always, *always*, in danger of losing our
poetry and honor. Every generation must do this work
again. Hillman's work is a Clarion Call for Christians,
for Catholics to recover our stories. And, oh, how we
need these stories! How they enrapture; elevate, inspire
and encourage, console and comfort us! What they tell
us—these stories about Samson, King David and finally
Christ and his disciples, Samson and Delilah and the
jawbone of an ass, and the bees that poured forth from
the lion's carcass, David the Shepherd boy slaying Goliath, and playing his harp for the King, about the birth
of the baby Jesus, the shepherds and the Wise Men, the
baptism by John the Baptist, the temptation in the Desert,
healing the sick, raising the Dead, preaching to the five
thousand, the Last Supper, the Crucifixion and Resur-

rection—is that God is like us, and that we honor Him, by increasing in Wisdom, but most of all in Love, Faith, Hope and Love, Hope and Charity, as St. Paul describes the supernatural virtues, about how though I speak with the tongues of Angels but have not Love, I am nothing.

And I would add to this precisely those writers Dr. Cowan listed to whose names I would add Bernanos, Sigrid Undset, and even Cormac MacCarthy.

A Catholic psychology that goes whoring after the false gods of science, the dehumanization of the fullness, of the depth and heights, the multi-dimensionality of our humanity; after what can be researched, proven, demonstrated, established, by the reductive methods of science, especially, in psychology—if engineers were held to the same standards of proof that scientific psychologists are, planes would be dropping daily from the sky; the "respectability" that both Faulkner and Bernanos knew to be the real menace to Christian Man, is to my mind, nothing short of an abject, inexcusable disgrace.

Catholic psychology can recover its soul through recourse to Hillman's psychology, to a soul, I repeat, always on the verge of being lost, a soul, primordially ordained to Truth and Goodness and Beauty. Psychology must pour forth these things, as if from an overflowing chalice, in every paper, in every book, lecture, conference, and, above all, with every patient. Truth is beauty, beauty is truth, that may not be all we need to know in Life, but we need to know it. As von Balthasar insists, beauty is that without which, the *sine qua non*, that truth loses its "cogency" and goodness its "savor." "Beauty," he says,

"is the disinterested one . . . a word which both imperceptibly and yet unmistakably, has bid farewell to our
new world, a world of interests, leaving it to its own avarice and sadness." Without beauty—do you recall your
Hopkins?—"*The world is charged with the grandeur of
God. / It will flame out, like shining from shook foil; it
gathers to a greatness, like the ooze of oil / Crushed . . .
There lives the dearest freshness deep down things / Because the Holy Ghost over the bent / World broods with
warm breast and with ah / bright / wings*—without the
beauty, the gasp, the poetry of radiance that James Hillman so singularly and so stunningly and so repeatedly
calls to our attention, psychology ceases to be worthy of
its calling.

One way to sum up Hillman's work is to say that he
honored psychology, honored its calling, his calling, his
vocation, that he grew downward, walking his splendid talk in the *The Soul's Code*, living it, embodying it,
becoming more and more, not what he was, but what
psychology is, must be, what psychology *must* become:
a Daimon, an Angel, a voice, a discipline, a craft, an ar-
resting force of some magnitude, even majesty, a force,
a voice that doesn't say, "No" as did Socrates' daimon,
but that says "Yes"; roars, "Yes!," the Saint with the
Lion, the Lion in the Desert, the Thought of the Heart, in
celebration of the Soul; to *personifying*—we come closest
to the psychological by personifying, said that marvelous
Lady Lou Andreas Salome; to *pathologizing*—Husserl
knew as did Faulkner and Bernanos that we encounter
essences only by deformation, by going to extremes;
by *dehumanizing*—the air is awash with Angels. As
St. Thomas said—and I quote; "all corporeal things are

governed by the angels. And this is not only the teaching of the holy doctors, but of all the philosophers." And Evil prowls about the earth just as surely as when slave ships packed with suffering victims regularly crossed the Atlantic and the Camps and Gulags murdered millions; by *seeing through or soul-making*, a Faulknerian, Hopkins- and Bernanos-like, schooled through them, by them, psychological *eye* for shadow and sudden shining splendor. That, finally, says "Yes!" poetically, rhetorically, rhapsodically, or, in Hillman's words, "with a language schooled and fashioned, though not fashioned in schools," to being human, to being all-too-human in a dangerous time in a beautiful world, where for psychology, thanks to the magisterial work of this one man, a psychologist and psychology truly worthy of the name, morning may finally have broken.

Bibliography

This is a selected bibliography relevant to the formation and development of the viewpoint represented here.

For the spiritual part of spiritual existentialism, I think the Bible and Blake and all the great high romantic poets can hardly be improved on.

Existentialism is such a wide umbrella—the best introduction, to my mind, is William Barrett's *Irrational Man* (New York: Doubleday, 1958). The single existentialist thinker who most influenced me is Paul Tillich. See *The Courage to Be* and his several books of sermons. Also, I admire Rollo May's exceptional humanity, intelligence and style.

As to Husserl, Heidegger and Merleau-Ponty, I studied them until I dropped while a student, and as Yeats said, "Truth flourishes where the student's lamp has shone."

For the Southern background, William Faulkner is essential, especially *Light in August* and his great trilogy, *The Hamlet; The Town;* and *The Mansion,* about the disgrace and destruction of the soul of the South, the killing of the mockingbird, through the evils of the Snopes family, Snopes being an anagram for $OPEN$, through a tentacular Calvinism and rampant commercialism and greed. See also Marshall McLuhan's "The Southern Quality" in *The Literary Criticism of Marshall McLuhan* (New York, McGraw-Hill, 1969).

Celtic consciousness may be appreciated through *The Celtic Consciousness*, edited by Robert O'Driscoll (New York: George Braziller, 1981, in limited edition of 500 copies by McClelland and Stewart and the Dolmen Press, 1982, by George Braziller). This is a mammoth collection of papers presented at a University of Toronto conference in celebration of the Celtic heritage. The bibliographies are exhaustive.

I am also deeply indebted to John Prebble's two books, *Glencoe* and *Culloden*, which in addition to being irreplaceable histories are also stunning literary achievements. I have used the Folio Editions.

For Hans Urs von Balthasar, see *The Glory of the Lord: A Theological Aesthetics,* Volumes I through VII, (San Francisco: Ignatius Press, 1989). Also *Man in History: A Theological Study* (London: Sheed and Ward, 1968, 1981). Very helpful as well is a lengthy review that can serve as an accessible introduction to von Balthasar by Robert E. Wood "Philosophy, Aesthetics and Theology: A Review of Hans Urs von Balthasar's *The Glory of the Lord* in *The American Catholic Philosophical Quarterly*, Volume LXVII, Summer 1983, No. 3, 355-383.

My favorite Greeley novel and the one to which his essay "Why Catholics Stay Catholics?—Because of the Stories" is appended in *White Smoke* (New York: Tom Doherty and Associates, 1996), but Greeley is prolific and everything he has written is worth reading. I'm partial to his novel *An Occasion of Sin*, a wonderful meditation through fiction on the meaning of sainthood.

Hillman's best two works *Revisioning Psychology* and *The Myth of Analysis*, both of which have been recently reprinted in new editions—*Revisioning* has an expanded introduction by Harper & Row. *The Soul's Code* (Random House, 1997) is by far Hillman's most popular book. *Bluefire*, an anthology of his writings edited by Thomas Moore is also a good place to start. But Hillman, like Greeley, is incredibly prolific and almost everything is valuable.

The two classic books on psychotherapy that I return to obsessively are Carl Roger's *Client-Centered Therapy* (New York: Houghton Mifflin, 1951, 1965) and Jay Haley's *Uncommon Therapy: The Psychiatric Techniques of Milton Erickson*, (New York, Norton, 1973).

For an overview of recent trends see *The Evolution of Psychotherapy: The United Conference*, edited by Jeffrey K. Zeig (New York: Brunner-Mazel, 1997).

Also throughout my development as a therapist, I've turned again and again to Alfred Adler, whom I've studied for twenty years, on whom I did my dissertation and a few other publications.

Regrettably, Adler's work is not so easy to get hold of. His truly magisterial *The Neurotic Character*, which to my mind is one of the best psychology books ever written, and a very helpful compilation of his case histories collected under the title of *Problems of Neurosis* (London: Kegan Paul, 1929), tend to be available only in libraries.

When I have taught therapy, to the Rogers and Erickson I've added Minuchin's, *The Family Kaleidoscope*, which is always the most popular text. Malone and Whitaker's *The Roots of Psychotherapy* (New York: Brunner Mazel, 1980) and Satir's *Conjoint Family Therapy* (Palo Alto: Science and Behavior Books, 1964), each extremely valuable, and all "directive" or "interventive" in approach. Each has a high intensity, quirky, full court press, offside kick, squeeze play kind of style.

Analytic, both Freudian and Jungian, disquisitions of therapeutic process and technique I avoid like the plague, primarily because they mystify a process so fundamentally human that our natural tendency to over-complicate it requires that therapy be reinvented time and time again in a more down to earth, human, common-sense form.

As a young counselor comparing myself to analysts who cultivated this mystique, always speaking about analysis in a hushed, reverential tone, I was paralyzed, and being insufficiently "analyzed" myself, afraid to do, or more importantly, say anything to clients for fear I would make a "technical error" and damage them.

Eventually like Adler I made my exit, so to speak, from Freud's Wednesday Night Circle and escaped from Jung's Burgholzi asylum, and, again like Adler, headed for the coffee house and cafe to discover there that intimate conversation where you feel safe, liked, relaxed, and in the mood, in addition to being just good fun, can be cathartic, instructive, educational, inspirational, a stimulus to love and creativity and eros, and through these facilitations, heal.

Eric Havelock's *Preface to Plato* (New York: Grosset & Dunlap, 1963), mainly his chapter on "The Psychology of the Poetic Performance," I reread almost monthly. For an almost ideogrammatic marvel of compression of the place and meaning of "preaching" within the oratorical tradition see Garry Wills, *Certain Trumpets: The Call of Leaders,* (New York, Simon & Schuster, 1994), pp. 197-211. Max Weber's analysis of Calvinism in *The Protestant Ethic and the Spirit of Capitalism*, translated by Talcott Parsons (New York: Charles Scibner's Sons, 1958) is original and true. I've also profited greatly from Camille Paglia, her masterwork *Sexual Personae*, together with her several collections of essays. Ms. Paglia's romantic realism, the Renaissance conversational wit and vigor of her turbo-fired prose style, but chiefly, her "essentialist" broadsides against the "constructivism" and "de-constructivism" that would deny the "extramentality," the power and objectivity of nature and human nature—the eros, violence and beauty—are marvels each.

A final comment, in response to the question most frequently asked by colleagues who read the earlier drafts of this manuscript, which was "Where would you put spiritual existentialism on the spectrum of contemporary counseling models?"—and from which they would not swerve despite the contentious expression of my dislike of systematics and my belief that systematics, in every form, with their necessary abstractions and totalizations, are more likely to obscure the beauty and meaning of experience rather than illumine it. Authentic enlightenment rewards a more phenomenological, intuitive, counseling-based approach. And since my answer both surprised and stimulated a very productive vein of talk, I conclude with it. It's with the Circus Animals, so to speak, rather than the foul rag and bone shop of the heart, that I exit.

In its emphasis on integration and synthesis, my approach is very definitely akin to the "synthetic eclecticism" championed by authors such as J.O. Prochaska and C.C. DiClemente—see their *The Transtheoretical Approach: Crossing Traditional Boundaries of Therapy* (Homewood, IL. Dow-Jones-Irwin, 1984) and Prochaska's *Systems of Psychotherapy* (Homewood, IL. Dorsey Press, 1984) and L.E. Beutler, *Eclectic Psychotherapy: A Systematic Approach* (New York: Pergamon, 1983)—and to the narrative therapies.

Synthesis, from my point of view, retains a very special meaning, drawn from existential Thomism, which is that "synthesizing" is the act within the mind that analogically mirrors or reflects the act of existing in the real. Thus any authentic "existential" psychology must be synthetic if it is to be faithful to reality. Further, I would argue that a synthetic approach to counseling is the most responsible and effective clinical posture because it frees a counselor from what can be the occasional unnecessary clinical constraints that are the price of strict adherence to any school or system. The fact is, however, that most counselors in their actual practice are far more flexible and eclectic than the theoretical system to which they adhere would allow.

The distinctions between spiritual existentialism and the eclectic and narrative therapies can be clarified in terms of both epistemology and metaphysics.

My epistemology is a critical realism. I adhere to a "truth as revelation" position and thus ally myself with the eclectics and against the constructivist, post-modernist and deconstructivist epistemologies that both underlie and inspire the narrative therapies. For an examination of these issues see Barbara S. Held, *Back to Reality: A Critique of Postmodern Theory in Psychotherapy* (New York: Norton, 1995). For a spirited defense of phenomenological-existentialism as a critical realism see Don Ihde's *Existential Technics* (Albany: SUNY Press, 1983 pp. 159-183). Ihde says, "At ground level the phenomenological army stands behind a battleflag which carries the motto, 'to the things themselves.' Often cited, this motto does implicitly contain an entire phenomenological program. First, there must be *things*. And in spite of the fact that the founder of phenomenology characterized his philosophical position as transcendental idealism, there remained within the diverse development of phenomenology a kind of *realist* emphasis. Writ large and reinterpreted as a totality, it is the World and it is always the World with which phenomenology begins and from which descriptive analysis springs."

As a Catholic existentialist I have also been heavily influenced by Thomistic epistemology. See Jacques Maritain's *Degrees of Knowledge*, but especially his chapter "The Liberation of the Intelligence" in his *The Peasant of the Garonne* (New York: Macmillan, 1968).

However, I would distinguish critical realism from the naïve, or scientific realism, which seems to me the basic epistemology informing the eclectic approach most of whose representative voices appear to believe in "truth as correspondence."

Further distinctions can be made by recourse to metaphysics, and the three transcendentals, Truth, Goodness and Beauty, to which, in a specifically Catholic existentialist perspective, I believe that all human existence is primordially oriented.

It seems to me that the fundamental contribution of the narrative therapies is the introduction into clinical theory of Beauty, that is, of an aesthetically inspired epistemology which defines truth in aesthetic terms—"truth as coherence," that is to say, an intervention, interpretation, or "narrative" has value according to traditional aesthetic criteria of complexity, irony, harmony, balance, form, symmetry, depth, intensity, "inscape," as the poet Hopkins would have described it.

Beauty also orients spiritual existentialism. I follow von Balthasar in his contention that Beauty is at the center of the transcendentals and that in the absence of beauty. Truth, as he says, loses its "cogency" and Goodness its "savor."

Thus spiritual existentialism converges with the narrative therapies in accepting and applying aesthetic and rhetorical criteria and categories to clinical interventions or narratives, and differs from the eclectics on precisely this ground. Few representatives of the eclectic orientation would accept aesthetic criteria for determining the most effective clinical intervention.

Put it this way: the eclectics might argue that an intervention is a good one because it is true, while the narrative therapists might argue that an intervention, a new narrative, is "true" once because it is beautiful, and in this way shows "narrative fidelity." I would argue that for an intervention to succeed, it must also to some degree be both true and beautiful.

But not quite, not quite. We also need the Good; we need ethics. Indeed the field of ethics provides the easiest way to distinguish the three truth theories we have described. Behind what was once called "situational ethics" but which I would prefer to call "existential ethics," is the "truth as revelation" idea. The right thing to do in any particular situation, or the right thing to say, which is my version of what the eclectics call the "matrix question" emerges from close, committed, phenomenological consideration of its human context, which, because of the nature of our humanity, always opens into spiritual and transcendental considerations. There is no single morality, no set of rule-governed and replicable norms, capable of being applied universally to every situation without regard for circumstance. To argue that such a set of rules or normals exists assumes a naïvely realist or "truth as correspondence" epistemology. In other words the right thing to do is simply what the rules tell you to do. But existential ethics does not imply relativism. One is not free to do simply whatever one pleases, or if we applied the "truth as coherence" criteria, that is, aesthetic criteria only, one is not free to do what one pleases so long as it is pleasing, that is, done with grace, style, intelligibility, and consistency.

If we eliminate the Good from counseling, that is to say, if we eliminate ethical considerations and apply only aesthetic ones, we inevitably end with some version of "style is all," if you do it with style, it's OK. The good narrative is the one that shows the most stylistic coherence and complexity. Yet if you admit both the True and the Beautiful, you will inevitably opt for some "master narrative," which asserts a truth value, that is, it says something true about life, "true-er" than alternative narratives.

My "master-narrative" is my Catholic faith. I believe. I believe in the Sacraments. I believe in the Saints. As Bernanos says: "We hold the temporal heritage of the saints. For there were blessed along with us the corn and the wine, the stone of our thresholds and the roof where the dove builds her nest; with us were blessed our poor beds full of dreams and forgetfulness; the highroad down which the country carts go squeaking; the young men with their pitiless laughter, and the maidens weeping at the fountains brink. And ever since then—even since God himself has visited us—is there anything in this world which our saints should not have taken back: is there anything at all which they cannot give?"

My admiration for Hillman is rooted in my Catholic faith. Indeed, I would argue, provocatively and intemperately, Bernanos style, that one cannot fully understand Hillman's lifelong martial defense of the soul—shall we call it "brave-hearted"?—unless one is Catholic. If the Renaissance was a return to the pagan gods, it was a *Catholic* return. A true Renaissance psychology in the sense that Hillman called for and practiced is perforce Catholic.

About the Author

Randolph W. Severson, Ph.D., is a counselor and writer. An early student and assistant to James Hillman, he holds a doctorate in existential-phenomenological psychology from the Institute of Philosophic Studies at the University of Dallas.

www.ingramcontent.com/pod-product-compliance
Lightning Source LLC
Chambersburg PA
CBHW032059080426
42733CB00006B/338